Staying SANE
the MUSIC game

BRETT LEBOFF

TABLE OF CONTENTS

TABLE OF CONTENTS continued

TABLE OF CONTENTS continued

PREFACE:

In 2016 an academic research paper was published by Music Tank at Westminster University. It stated:

A recent University of Westminster pilot survey of 2,211 self-identifying professional musicians working across a broad swathe of the UK music industry found that:

- *71% of respondents believed they had experienced incidences of anxiety and panic attacks*
- *68% of respondents experienced incidences of depression*

Office for National Statistics data (2010-13) indicated that nearly 1 in 5 of the population suffer from anxiety and/or depression (aged 16 years +). **This research suggests that musicians could be up to three times more likely to suffer from depression compared to the general public.**

(Gross and Musgrave 2016 Music Tank)

Research funded by Help Musicians UK.

I have been in the music industry the whole of my adult life, firstly as a drummer, then as a manager and now as a coach/consultant.

I have seen the same patterns emerging time and time again. Musicians suffering from a life going against the grain. Living the unconventional, living on the edge and in the unknown, which is a necessary space from which to create art. It can be a warrior's life, a life of constant battle and challenges that show themselves so starkly.

Having lived this for 20 years, I have seen these same themes come up with hundreds of musicians who have a propensity for depression and look to drink and drugs to escape.

Some have figured it out, some haven't, some have died... I have gone through similar patterns in my life, but over the last 6 years, I have been making it my priority to investigate tools that work and can transform the lives of musicians, and music industry professionals, to help them come out of those cycles.

I would not still be here, working in this industry and finding my happiness increasing every day, if it were not for the tools found in this book.

I believe that the tools and philosophies found here can contribute to musicians and industry professionals leading much healthier, functional lives, whilst being able to access a deeper connection to creativity; running richer, sustainable careers and still having fun!

INTRODUCTION:

I am a HUGE Michael Jackson fan since the age of around 11. I mean, massive! I have most books about him, watched the movies, interviews, countless gigs, seen him live, bought the merchandise etc. How many times did he sing about us being the best humans we can possibly be? How many times did he talk about the depth of love and the human experience and other meaningful virtues?

From what I understand of him though, it is clear the guy was a nasty businessman, lacked loyalty to those close to him and screwed people over countless times. I mean, really, immoral. He f***ed his friends over, he was vicious and dog eat dog when it came to his profile, career and anything involving money. One example – he asked Paul McCartney, who was a very good friend of his, how he should invest his money. Paul told him to invest in music publishing, it was an asset and he could make money buying up song rights. The next day, he bought the Beatles catalogue! BOUGHT IT ALL! Crazy hey? Apparently Greg Phillinganes his musical director and keyboard player for most of his career, had co-written a lot for which he was not paid or even credited. I am not in the business of stamping on a great entertainer's grave, *but* this illustrates a clear point. MJ did not live by the virtues of the songs he sung. Which then suggests a lack of integrity as a human being. I have always believed that art and artist should be separated, because we are all human and we mess up and make mistakes. However, what if you as an artist could aspire and try to live by the virtues expressed in your existence as a musician and if you did, would it have profound effects on your mental health…?

What fundamentals make good music? I would say, at least the following:

- Great communication between each musician
- Understanding complicated concepts on a deep level
- The ability to make something from nothing
- Being an adventurous explorer
- Having the strength to go to the edge and return – very regularly!
- Inquisitiveness
- Empathy
- Heightened awareness
- Self-awareness
- Space
- A sense of timeless expression
- An appreciation of the unfathomable/ineffable powers that exist in the universe
- To see the unseen and name it
- To speak the unsaid
- To call people out on their bullshit in a loving, beautifully creative way
- To write, sing and play about your own struggles
- To form unbelievably close bonds with random humans,

very quickly who get all this stuff
- Communicating on a deep level with people you don't know so well and those you do

So these are tools and patterns that, as a musician, you use all the time and are, I would suggest, a musician's natural state. Acting in these ways above brings you to a natural, happy place, where you feel aligned and integrated as a human.

So here's the question and the theory... What happens when you lack integrity and do not use these tools in your daily life, or live as you know you can in your naturally expressed state? I think you become sad, depressed, hide your true self, and can suck the joy out of your existence. This is because you are a high-level being that can live in all the attributes above, so that when you don't, you are truly screwing yourself over and on a deep down level, you know it!

I put it to you, that because you know on a deep level, you are living in bullshit, it kills you. You see your darkness, you see your light. You are capable of living in a high-level truth. You need to be inspired to live like that and this book will help you.

The reason you are so happy when you play music, feel it helps your mental health and your ability to live in your best self is because you are bringing your truth. If you start using all those qualities and bringing that awareness and those gifts to your day-to-day life then you will achieve a much higher happiness. When you do that, you will be living your truth. SO why not make your human, everyday life and interactions away from your instrument/creations, as sincere, as fully

> **I want to help you open up another way of being... let's explore how to do it healthily, sustainably and from your higher self...**

focused, as visionary and full of love as you make your music.

Creating and playing music is a spiritual practice. But as a creator you also have to go into battle, so like a warrior, you need to take some armour, or you're going to get hurt.

Music is an unexplainable force and can be likened to the way people describe God. To deny that would be to deny music its mystical powers – connection, transcendence and its ability to cut through and communicate with our deepest selves.

Just as we can take a spiritual practice like sex and make it animalistic, we can take music and make it base. We can make music formulaic and purposely trick people's minds and invite them into its familiarity, which is what the pop music industry has often done – and does – particularly in our age of electronics.

At its essence, realised correctly, in whatever genre, music has the ability to speak to our core, our souls, on a deep level, like love.

Therefore, it follows that in order to do that should not the creator of the music be able to access a higher state, before writing the music?

I will present the case in this book that as a musician, you may well be *using* music to help raise your spiritual level; that when you play/sing/create music you find yourself accessing what we will call 'the zone'. What happens to the quality of art that is created if you are in a higher place – 'the zone' –

when you start creating it? Imagine if your mind is clear and completely focused when you sit down to create.

I want to help you open up another way of being, one that means you really get the best out of all the work that needs to happen, one that relieves you of the unnecessary anxiety and stress that can plague anyone living on the edge, constantly venturing into the unknown. I want to recognise that you are a superhero of life, constantly exploring that which many are too afraid to. You have ignored numerous friends, parents, teachers and those who think they know what is best for your life. You have heroically chosen a path that you know intrinsically you need to take. You have sacrificed the earlier opportunities you had to accumulate wealth, stability and 'respect'. I celebrate your choice – it is not an easy path to take – and let's be honest, what else would you do that makes you happy? With this in mind, let's explore how to do it healthily, sustainably and from your higher self, rather than from a place of desperation.

This book will go through aspects of your life as a musician and help you to put in place systems that will aid you to navigate the torrid waters of trying to live from your art – the conundrum that is music meeting business. I am not going to deal with 'how to make it in the music industry', although, I will strongly argue that if you follow the guidance of this book it will give you longevity – the ability to continue pushing forward, becoming more productive, happier and more creative.

Great artists normally embody their art, live on the edge, express the unknown and examine deeply because they have some level of torment. I don't believe that we can remove that torment completely, especially if it is historical, though we can at least explore patterns that have developed, create awareness around them and therefore make steps to implement change. If the suffering that you experience is a part of your past then you are probably acting on patterns you built as a defence against that suffering that may not be useful to you anymore. Using examples, we will explore the patterns of your life as a musician and how you are contributing to your problems. At every juncture we will look at how and what changes can be implemented to help create a new, sustainable structure for your day-to-day life. It is my belief that by creating awareness and changes in your life, you will be able to observe your agony, struggles and challenges from a different perspective, let's say an 'aerial viewpoint'. This will give you wisdom and understanding, and will add to your creative being, allowing you to create from a 'higher self'.

The trick to today's industry is having staying power; it can take 10-15 years to forge a stable, professional career in today's music industry; that is often 10 years without proper money, meaning you are either extremely poor or have to work another job at the same time. Once you are professional, given the investment of time and sacrifice, it would be beneficial to have a life structure that sustains your career for as long as possible.

The beginning of the book will teach you something I call the Zone Technique, to which we will continually refer. The rest of the book deals with all aspects of your lifestyle, career and creativity. The Zone Technique will quite simply help you reach the 'zone' that you are familiar with when everything is going well for you, when on stage or in practice, and you feel at peace. It is that timeless place, where everything just feels and sounds right. You may well have your eyes shut, or just be lost in the music, sound and groove that you, and those around you, are creating and you are hearing.

Let's speak of this 'zone' you are already familiar with from practising and being on stage.

Olympic athletes can access it as can someone doing the gardening. It is a meditative space where the human is accessing a deep, spiritual flow. The conscious mind is silent; the subconscious is guiding it the way it knows best. At its best and deepest, there is a feeling of complete peace and calm. For those who have taken Ecstasy, then perhaps the feeling can be likened to doing a form of 'Ecstasy lite' for the first time! BUT, you can access this feeling time and time again, completely consciously. Therefore, it is sustainable, free of charge and I am also able to guide you through this.

Imagine if you could reach a peaceful 'flow state' *before* picking up your instrument, singing or writing? What would that achieve when you actually do go into your creative space? I understand that sometimes, *using* music to express a deep anguish can lead to immense creations. I am not suggesting that this is invalid, but I do suggest that accessing a higher spiritual plane before creating will never forgo the inspiration you had for writing in the first place. If anything, it will add perspective and levels that you never thought you could access.

You will not have any trouble accessing 'the zone' away from your instrument or creating and using the techniques in Chapter 2 reasonably quickly in

> **Let's speak of this 'zone' you're already familiar with from practising and being on stage...**

15

comparison with anyone else. You will certainly recognise it when you get there. This can be a EUREKA moment. I will then invite you to access that place for a short time before you enter the creative space.

What I like to call Zone Technique is quite simple really, as a concept: concentrate wholly on something, one thing, focus absolutely intensely, without trying to change anything. As you are focusing only on one thing, observing, without trying to change it, you are practising how to bring yourself to a state of inner peace. It is a practice that quietens the mind, and the more you do it the deeper you can go. Wise masters and people have been practising this kind of thing for thousands of years. It is a natural state for humans to access; it is a place of peace and quiet, a total escape from mind chatter. As I said, you have already been doing this and I predict that your entry into 'the zone' will be swifter and easier than those who have not been there much before, if at all!

The practice of bringing yourself into a state of peace, being distracted, and then bringing yourself back to the zone again, is a tool that you will be able to use throughout various areas of your life. You can then become skilled at being able to float away into a state of bliss, only feeling that exact moment. Getting used to being distracted away from this bliss state, whilst then being able to float back again, without feeling pain, frustration or anger, will make you such a strong person that you will see the positive repercussions across every part of your existence.

At the beginning you may go to 'the zone' and then hear mind chatter again. With the guidance in this book, you will learn to bring yourself back to 'the zone', again you may get distracted and again you will learn to bring yourself back to 'the zone'. THIS is actually the true practice of Zone Technique. The more you do this, the more readily available access to 'the zone' will be. I have been using this technique for a long time, and still if my practice slips for a few days, my mind feels cluttered, very busy and messy. It can often take a much longer session to bring my mind back. BUT, 'the zone' is always there to touch, even if I do not remain there long, the practice of noticing being distracted and then going back in (with the techniques I will show you), is in itself such a valuable exercise, which still cosmically clears the mind and allows space. If you are confused by my explanations, don't worry, we will work through the technique with much more explanation in Chapter 2.

Muhammad Ali said: "Only a man who knows what it is like to be defeated can reach down to the bottom of his soul and come up with the extra ounce of power it takes to win when the match is even."

It's a cliché, and we have all heard it before, but I have a bit of a different take on it... A little cheesy poem, if you will:

You will fail,
You will fall,
BUT JUST by getting back up AGAIN
You're stronger than before!

So, this book is a resource to help the musicians/composers/singers/producers attain a deeper spiritual level of consciousness. Instead of just using the instrument, voice or creations to attain a higher level of meaning, I will state the case that the creator is able to access a deeper level of spirit before entering the creative process, so that the responsibility of creation is taken more seriously and that the preparation

17

helps unlock a deeper perspective found inside your soul.

As an artist today you need to do what artists do best, which is to embody the chaos and out of that chaos, create order. You need to battle with your greatest fears of constantly stepping into the unknown, to express yourself on the rest of society's behalf that which is not spoken. But, you also need to have your hand on your business. After being in the chaotic space, you need to be at the meeting at 10 a.m., on time, with a smile on your face, or the people who will help run your business won't work with you!

There are high demands on an artist's life in the 21st century. We will explore ways of dealing with your unconventional lives, interactions within bands, rehearsals, attitude to recording, live gigs, potential business partners; finding ways of staying sane in all areas of your work, so that your productivity and happiness is increased exponentially. I will also give you tools to avoid needing to constantly turn to drugs/alcohol, inflate your ego or other vices as an escape from yourself and to disconnect and escape from your truth.

I spent my teenage years around music a lot, at school, then my older brother brought me into his covers band when I was 14 and the other guys were years older, because their drummer was unreliable (much better than me though!). Before I even got into the band, because they often rehearsed at our house, I would sit and watch them practise, dreaming of getting on the drum stool. I improved a lot in a short space of time, mainly because of the embarrassment of being that much worse than the others drove me on and made me rehearse. I used the fear and the pressure to drive forward and have either continued in this vein throughout my life, or run away to escape the pressure. Two complete extremes! I believe I have pushed both extremes to such limits and seen everything in between that I have attained an understanding of what I see as 'universal law'. I am not a professor, I have learned from experience. I have always experimented with pushing the envelope of possibilities in life as far as possible! Much to the frustration of friends, colleagues, parents and teachers, I have rarely lived by any rules, other than those defined by myself. Due to the amount of time I spent with musicians, being one and then the time I have devoted in the business (more than 10 years in each realm), I feel like I am sitting on a high wall, legs dangling down each side. On one side, the musicians, dancers, actors, artists, magicians and on the other side the straighter people, business people, organised people, disciplined and mainstream people. I understand both perspectives, I can see the challenges that exist and appreciate the life choices of both. I feel like I have gained an aerial viewpoint – the helicopter, the high wall perspective. All of this, including struggling with the extreme myself, watching the insanity that can be created in artists' minds, as well as having done a lot of work on myself, made me write this book. It felt like the next natural step in my life.

In music you learn all the theory and then you throw away the rules and break them. I think the same is needed for a musicians' everyday life. You need to be offered a structure for every avenue of your daily life and then, as a creative being, you will learn to break those rules and adjust them for you as an individual. To my knowledge, nothing like this has been suggested and there is no blueprint life structure for a musician to use as a guide. Therefore, I offer my knowledge of this esoteric and unconventional life a musician has to endure and give my suggested life plan, which I expect you to modify and change to suit you as an individual.

Perhaps, in years to come, this will affect the output of musicians all over the world and may even have a significant impact, disrupting the airwaves and 'stream waves'.

You are about to enter a journey of technique, philosophy and musical life stories. With these, it will be possible to transform both your creative and life experience.

The last thing I need to say is instructive – THIS IS NOT A PASSIVE BOOK. You cannot just read it and expect magic results. There are many parts of the book that demand your involvement with learning techniques, practising and implementing change, and new models and ways of running your life. Reading it and putting it on your shelf will probably make little difference to your life.

BUT, speaking from experience, THE GUARANTEE IS that if you implement the ideas in this book, they will have profound effects on your life, your career and your happiness. I can absolutely guarantee that it WILL change your life if you follow it.

However, I know that as a musician, one of your strengths is to bend the rules, learning the structures and using them, but also existing outside of those rules and bringing your creative mind to shape your own path, both musically and your day-to-day life. As we journey together, you will find each chapter goes deeper. I invite you to take the ideas and play with them, use this as a suggested structure, like the theory of music, and of course see these rules as malleable and adjustable for your life as an individual as you see fit.

"Music is emotion *and* science."
Quincy Jones (Interview by David Marchese for Vulture.com Feb 2018)

CHAPTER 1

The Struggle of Being an Aspiring or Pro Musician

The zone is a place of no conscious thought. It is a place where subconscious energy flows and things that you have learnt to hide away, flow out. It is a place that worries and anxiety cannot touch, a place where truth, light and your wisest energy resides.

The zone is somewhere that you go when you are playing or singing an amazing solo. The zone is somewhere where you can have an out-of-body experience. The zone is your true expression and your true soul coming through.

Do you admire how pro PRINCE was as an artist? He was not superhuman; he was committed, talented and worked hard.

He just focused on music and made that his daily toil, probably for the majority of the hours he was awake all of his life. When you look at any artist who you admire like that, guaranteed it will be the same story. Just focus on what you want. Just spend your time doing what you want your life to be and eventually, through the struggles, it will happen.

He should be an inspiration to us all, musician or not. To follow your passion and do it the very best you possibly can.

I find him inspiring because he demonstrated what humans are capable of with focus and putting in the hours.

When I was a child I grew up in a dysfunctional family home. I will not go into detail, suffice it to say, when I tell my story it is up there with the most dysfunctional of childhoods all the way up to the age of 18. There was a lot of chaos, abuse, shouting, violence, sadness and commotion. I felt that I always needed to escape.

Thankfully, my mother insisted that I start learning to play piano when I was about seven years old. My grandfather was musical, playing the piano and violin and often singing in the operatic style. There was always loud music coming from his car. There was often music being played by family in the house. I am thankful for all the music that was in my life at a young age. By the time I was eleven, I realised that I wasn't connecting to the piano. Maybe I felt that it wasn't allowing me to express myself because of the way that my teacher approached playing the instrument.

Maybe it was the fact that my older brother played the piano; he was four years older than me, already playing songs and chords, and was the go-to guy for a sing-song! I have a memory of thinking *I'll never be as good as him!* So, I think I was already on the lookout for a new instrument! When I went to secondary school (high school) we were being shown around the music block and I remember seeing (and hearing) an older pupil through a small window, on the other side of a big, solid door, sitting behind the drum kit, smashing the drums and playing very loudly.

I remember looking at that big white drum kit through the small glass window that separated me from the tall teenager on those drums. All I remember thinking at that

> **At school I joined every band possible; the wind band, the brass band and the jazz band...**

moment was; *what the hell are those?* In a captivated stare, I knew, in that instance, in my mind, I had to play this instrument.

I went home to my mother and begged her to allow me to have drum lessons. Amazingly, within only a few weeks, I was signed up and ready to embark on the long road to playing the drums. The one condition that separated me from having a drum kit at home was that I had to do at least one year of lessons and there should also be a recommendation from my teacher before my mother would buy me a full kit.

I did my one year of lessons and, true to her word, my mum bought me my own drum kit. I LOVED IT!

We were fortunate enough to have a room just for music, which contained both a piano and drums. I remember going into that room on a daily basis, proudly sitting behind the drums, putting on the latest cassette (yes cassette!), plugging in my headphones and playing to my heart's content. When I arrived home from school, I played those drums every day.

I was fortunate that with all the problems in my family, and all the dysfunction, I was so blessed that my parents and siblings had no issue with me smashing the drums any time, which, looking back, is quite remarkable; I thank them all for this, as I am not sure I would have been as patient. It couldn't have sounded all that great!

At school I joined every band possible; the wind band, the brass band and the jazz band. I played drums in the morning before school, and during the school day I would often bunk lessons and pretend that I had a drum lesson – even though my drum teacher was only in school on certain days this seemed to work quite well! I went into the music block on a regular basis and played the drums sometimes for several hours a day. Looking back on those times, I realise now that when I was practising the same bar over and over again I was getting into what I would call 'the zone'.

You know that 'zone', I know you do! Well, to be introduced to that zone, at that time of my life, probably saved me. Can you say the same thing? It is my assumption that you may well have turned to music as a safe escape, a 'womb' if you like. Somewhere that you could create a safe space, where nothing could touch you. Well, this was, and still is, a special place for me. It is a place that brings peace, tranquillity and no questions. It is a place that is out of this world, which is hard to describe to anyone who has not visited it.

When I talk to teachers of yoga, when I talk to teachers of sports, music or any other discipline, it is clear that the zone exists in all of these activities.

In this book, amongst many other things, we are going to explore how to consciously reach the zone without your instrument, the singing, the writing or the creating. We will study techniques to enable you to access that zone, away from your musical discipline.

We will explore the zone so that you can access it consciously, at any time that you wish without your instrument, so that when you are creating you can use the clear, flow space to attain a purer spiritual level. Why? Because you will access your deepest creative juices; it will give you the power to create from your deepest 'highest self' – the wise self you love and know, on the occasions you are truly proud of yourself, the self you know you are embodying when you feel that you are living your true potential.

We will also learn how to access that zone in order to overcome the struggles that you face on a day-to-day basis as a professional musician or someone who would like to be a professional musician.

Personally, I don't think I was ever destined to be a professional musician in the long term. That became clear to me and I changed my path and went into management because I felt that I had more to offer as a facilitator than I did as a drummer. But now, on reflection and about 14 years after my relatively short professional drumming career, I realise that what that professional drumming helped me to do was unlock my deepest feelings and understandings, and it connected me to my deepest truth. It also showed me how incredibly hard it is to be a professional musician, how much dedication, sacrifice and focus is needed to sustain a successful career. What I didn't realise at the time I changed direction, is that the professional course on which I would decide – helping musicians in their business – would also take as much personal sacrifice and dedication as I would have needed to put into my career as a drummer! I have no regrets about this change and know that it was the correct decision for me, but I did dive into the business side blinded and ignorant!

When I was drumming daily, I reflect on the fact that, with entering into the zone on a daily basis, which, unknowingly, became a meditative practice, I realised some inexpressible truths. I also feel it saved my life and that perhaps, without that escape into the zone on a daily basis through the drums, I may not be here to tell this story and share with you the wisdom with which I have been gifted throughout my life.

We will return to parts of my journey later on, and only when it is relevant – this book is not about me. We will walk through my experiences as a pro musician, in original projects, as a session player and then draw on my management career, in order to visualise experiences as examples, as I have witnessed over and over again the stresses and struggles that aspiring and professional musicians have to face.

I have seen the same mistakes made time and time again – by artists who have raw talent but focus on the wrong things and bands who don't communicate properly. The challenges that bands have, as I see it, are, that unless you have representation, there is no specific guidance on offer about how to run your complicated lives. Nowadays there is no barrier to entry, whereas in the days when I started out record companies still controlled distribution. Now it's almost like you can record a track and a video in the morning and release it in the afternoon. But, when there is total freedom, you will often wonder where to start. The game has no rules any more, so you have to make up your own, which is much harder than playing a game where you follow strict rules.

I want to offer some wisdom to help calm the mind and the soul, and unlock the deepest creativity within you. This is in order to help you tell your 'truth' and feel good and happy about yourself, as well as work better with other musical

> **We will also learn how to access that zone in order to overcome the struggles that you face on a day-to-day basis...**

colleagues and gain the most from the various environments and situations in which you need to thrive.

As a musician who is aspiring to become professional, you are likely to face several struggles on a daily basis. These are:

- Anxiety
- Stress

Which can come from:

- The feeling of lack of control
- Financial pressures
- Lack of confidence/belief in yourself
- Feeling judged
- Working hard in a job to pay bills whilst trying to succeed. EVERYTHING IS TOO MUCH
- Pressure from friends and family who are always asking 'how is the music going?'
- Pressure from yourself
- Bad thoughts – way too many!

> *Anxiety also comes from taking the thoughts that come into your head and believing them...*

Some days you are overcome with anxious thoughts, e.g. *Will I ever get there? How will I get my music out? I have so much to say and yet no one wants to listen. Does anyone care what I have to say? Is it that important anyway? Why do I have this drive to do this? Wouldn't it be better if I just had a regular wage, settled down with someone and maybe have a family...? Why am I not happy doing that anyway?*

I think anxiety is the feeling that you get when you are not living in your own truth. I know that my anxious thoughts often come from trying to predict the future and not living in the now.

Anxiety also comes from taking the thoughts that come into your head and believing them, taking some ownership over them. You make the decision that, because you've been thinking them, they must be real and true to you. However, we all have thoughts like this, thoughts that are so self-deprecating that you get into a really dark space and have a low opinion of yourself. Terrible thoughts of doing terrible things; embarrassing thoughts of doing naughty things, mischievous thoughts, playful thoughts. The great thing about thoughts is you can decide to let them go, you do not need to take them on board as truth. I believe that thoughts are flowing through us all the time from a field of consciousness that, maybe, we don't yet understand.

The idea that these thoughts are then believed to be part of you and that they are YOUR thoughts is, in my opinion, false. Well, yes, you are not your thoughts, but you may own a thought. Picture the scene; it is your life… You are walking through life on a stony beach, there is beauty always to the left of you, and all you see is the expansiveness of the sea, the colour of the sky, hearing the sounds of the crashing waves. As you walk on the beach, you see a stone that speaks to you, it is heavy, and you walk with it for some time in your pocket. You don't really like this stone, but you have decided for some reason, almost unconsciously, to walk with it. A little further down the beach, after some considerable time, you find another stone, this one heavier than before, and you put that one in your pocket. You are feeling heavier. Before you have even given yourself a chance to consider how heavy these stones are, you see another stone and you are drawn to it. This stone is, perhaps, even larger than the one before. Without thinking anything more, you pick up the stone and add this one to the other stones in your pocket. This is almost becoming habitual now!

You continue picking up stones, putting them in your pocket. Sometimes you have a handful of stones that you pick up and drop in quick succession. Instead of looking at the beautiful ocean, listening to the sounds of seagulls, waves and seeing the sunshine, your gaze is entirely fixed on stones, picking up, pocketing, picking up, inspecting. You have been continuously picking up stones and putting them in your pocket for a long time now! The stones are in some way a part of you (they're in your pocket) but they are not actually you – you can drop them at any time! You can look at the sea, breathe and enjoy the view, whilst noticing the stones on the floor and acknowledging them, without picking them up and holding them, or putting them in your pocket! You can even pick up a stone, look at it and observe it, 'understand it' and then put it back down again! Same with a thought, for a brief time it is a part of you, but once you realise you don't NEED to identify with it, you can drop it and only then, it is truly separate from you.

Remember the phrase; WE ARE NOT OUR THOUGHTS.

We are not our thoughts.

You are not your thoughts.

You do not have to believe all of your thoughts.

Imagine you are at a gig; you are going to watch a friend's band. You know people at the gig, in fact, there are a few different 'crews' there that you can probably join. You go to the bar and, on your way, there are lots of smiles and 'hellos'. You give some hugs and some brief words whilst clearly heading to the bar. Whilst you are waiting, either consciously or subconsciously, you start filtering through all the various groups you have seen and start thinking about who you would really like to hang out with. By the time your drink is served, you have decided who you are going to approach.

It is YOUR choice. No one in the various groups cares that much who you go and hang with. You may have feelings that the other crews are judging you, but they are probably way too busy having fun for that. Either that or you are too caught up in your own inner thoughts. Basically, unless you are actually rude and totally and weirdly ignore all the other groups, you are free to choose who you want to spend time with. You may flit around a bit, because you want to have more of a chat with certain people. This is all YOUR CHOICE, it's your decision who you choose and who you don't.

Let's go one stage further. Let's say that you have chosen a group to settle in with for a bit and the conversation is going well, but then it takes a turn for the worse when the one person in the group, with whom you don't connect, starts to dominate the chat. You can see it is not going to change, so you decide to slip off and go to another group of people. There is NO problem with this, right? This is standard behaviour and actually, healthy behaviour, because you are looking after your needs and it is not to the detriment of others.

Now let's go back to your thoughts. When thoughts come into your head, how about trying this exercise; you observe your thoughts (you can even have a very close look, briefly!) and once you understand the thought – having observed and probably not needed very long – it is completely YOUR CHOICE whether to dwell further on that thought or let it go. Our brains are so powerful you can decide in milliseconds if that thought is useful or not. You can decide if it is fantasy, fear, real or necessary to act on. All manner of action can be decided in a second. If you are not sure you can dwell for a bit until you understand it better. Try to understand where it is coming from. If it is any of the challenges that I have listed earlier in this chapter, it would be my advice to create awareness about where that thought comes from – perhaps it is a voice from a family member, a voice from someone that you have held on to for far too long and it is time to let go?

If it is a thought that is recurring, then why? We will deal in this book, with many of the challenging thoughts you have and try and help to shine a light on their origin. I encourage you to try and dissect where the thoughts are coming from – perhaps childhood experiences, defence mechanisms you built up which you needed and which played a real role in your life but are no longer necessary. Once you understand where the thought comes from, you can really decide to let it go. As a very general rule, I would classify any derogatory thoughts as ones that are not useful UNLESS there is a specific action that can be taken to rectify it.

For example: I am feeling like I am totally useless because my creative productivity is non-existent. Action: to sit at the piano and start playing some covers or old songs and see if

I start getting inspired. This is definitely the better option, instead of skinning up a reefer and sitting exploring why I am such a useless bastard and my creative juices aren't flowing! Otherwise, start focusing on OBSERVING thoughts, without action. Until you understand them and then either LET IT GO, or act on that thought. You need to assess if it is really beneficial to you now, and that you can truly justify it, from a place of your inner truth.

The great thing about thoughts is that we can only hold one thought in our head at any one time, but they can move very quickly, so it feels like we are holding many thoughts. Actually this is not the case, it is only one thought at a time, however quickly they come. The thing to remember is that when you focus on a negative thought, it blocks the road for more thoughts to come. Imagine a contraflow on the motorway/highway. The traffic is down to one lane and then a big truck breaks down. The big truck represents the bad thought, all the other cars (thoughts) behind are backed up and can't reach you.

One of the things that takes you away from knowing which thoughts are useful and which thoughts are not, is a lack of being in touch with your true self. It is a lack of being able to understand what you truly believe in as a human. This means that when you think a thought, you can decide in your deepest core if it is a truth for you or not. Are you living in YOUR truth, not for someone else, or in someone else's truth? This can lead to making healthy or unhealthy decisions.

Perhaps your thought process has been influenced by the many people around you? Stories you hear and the idea that everything that you are doing, and the path that you are on, is wrong.

For example, I have drawn a mind map of all the ideas that I would like to express in this book. I am sitting here, writing the first chapter and my thoughts are starting to go *Wow! There are so many ideas here, how will I get them all down?*

Will I ever finish this book?

Will anyone ever read it anyway?

What if I don't save the work and I lose everything I've written up to this point?

This book is going to take ages to write; maybe this is even going to take two or three years?

Well, I am writing this book because I fully believe in the message that I am putting across to you. I am enjoying the process so far! I am combining almost all the knowledge I have gained through life so far, and it feels like this is truly and deeply my purpose right now. The feeling of living in your true purpose is, I think, unmistakable. I believe that there is nothing else available for musicians that will express the ideas in this book; that perhaps no one else in the world can write this book and express the ideas in here, particularly because of the combined elements, what I have learnt and my life experiences.

Shadow Work:

It is important at this point to mention 'shadow work'. It originates from the Jungian idea of the shadow. It also involves constellation work which originates from a shamanic tradition of healing. I have partaken in it and found it a cosmic practice that transformed my life experience. The concept is that we all have our shadows, which are attributes that we have grown with and developed throughout our lives.

In some cases, we have only aided their development. We are mostly fearful of them; we do not want to believe that we are capable of bad things. But, as humans, *we are* capable of evil and bad things. We try and hide our shadows, use the 'ostrich technique' of putting our head in the sand. The issue with this is that when we ignore something that is real it grows, and when it grows and we continue to ignore it, then it becomes a monster. Try and think of the most mundane things in your life, like the dirty washing pile in your room! Then think about driving along with hardly any petrol in the car or van. Any example of ignoring something that you know is wrong will only turn into a monster eventually. This is the same with the shadow. So, shadow work is about admitting our issues, knowing we have problems. We all have faults, we all have issues. Once we come to terms with that, and have the bravery to actually look at our shadows, examine them, we take them metaphorically from behind us, where they can control us without our awareness, and bring it/them right in front of our eyes. Only last night I had an interesting WhatsApp conversation with a good friend, who has been doing a lot of work on himself. I am fortunate enough to have contemporaries everywhere I look that are quite obsessed with self-improvement!

I want to include the WhatsApp conversation as it will demonstrate and give a real-life example of how we all have difficult thoughts, which we want to improve and refine, that you may find a synchronicity with how you feel. A realisation I had a

> **The feeling of living in your true purpose is, I think, unmistakable...**

35

few years ago, when I started doing group shadow work, is that EVERYONE has their shit. We all have problems, and we often think that loads of people don't. But one thing that links our human experience together is yes, we all have shit! For the sake of anonymity, we will call him Derek (this is a conversation with a man, when we get to the part of suggesting workshops there are women's alternatives too. Woman Within is the equivalent to the ManKind Project and there is a Women's Workshop and a Men's Workshop for The New Tantra):

Derek: All this Zone Technique and ego work has made me realise how fucked up I am. It's so hard for me to be at ease with just my mind and thoughts.

Me: I have been clean of fags and booze and all since 5th Jan, but had a few on Friday eve. It's nice when you just have one night every few weeks.

Derek: And hard to also be mindful! Constantly want to escape into addiction.

Me: So don't get down about it. Just stop again.

Derek: Or get lost in bad, deluded thoughts. Yeah maybe I will try and do that. But for me when I'm hung-over; it's like a mental breakdown! I literally feel completely mentally fucked.

Me: Yeh man, we all have that. I try and look outside of myself when that happens. Also exercise and just completely focusing on 'the other' really helps. It's hard.

Derek: For sure! But sometimes when lost in thought, it's so hard to come back to reality.

Me: We have been growing up in a hedonistic culture.

Derek: For sure.

Me: You can choose to let thoughts go.

Derek: A lot of the time, especially lately, thoughts which are not my thoughts come into my head.

Me: What you're talking about is training like any other training.

Derek: But, I have really stupid thoughts. Deluded thoughts. Scary thoughts.

Me: I would argue that thoughts are never YOUR thoughts. They come from outside of ourselves and you choose which ones to latch on to.

Derek: That's good to hear! Hopefully my mindfulness and not being so attached to thought and emotion will help over a length of time! Practice.

Me: Yeh man, it's like any other practice.

Derek: I think the anxious me latches on to the thoughts saying what I can't think like this, what's wrong with me and that just makes it worse.

Me: You should read about Jung's archetypes.

Derek: Will check that out.

Me: Learn about how to embrace your sovereign energy, as 'the king' you can choose to let thought go and you can chat to the different parts of yourself and 'rule your kingdom'.

Derek: My biggest fear is becoming psychotic like my brother and/or being that ill that I am suicidal.

Me: It's cosmic stuff.

Derek: But I think the problem is actually the fear of that! Like becoming my brother who is psychotic.

Me: Sorry to hear you have that challenge.

Derek: Yeah I need to somehow rule it.

Me: So when you spend that time worrying that you will become like that, the fear makes it grow.

Derek: Yep.

Me: I would suggest that you do some professional work.

Derek: What like?

Me: Either ManKind Project or The New Tantra Men's Workshop.

Derek: I think if I improve my routine and hobbies and interests more then the fear will be replaced with thinking about my interests etc.

Me: Yes that is true of course. But also having support. And also being in atmospheres realising that we all have had or face these issues. Research shadow work.

Derek: OK bro.

Me: What you are talking about is being scared of your shadow. We all have a shadow.

Derek: I know we all suffer but for some reason I still at times think and feel that I am truly the fucked up one.

Me: Once you bring that shadow around the front and face it with your eyes it won't have power over you. At the moment it is behind you. That's why you're scared of it. You need to bring hyper awareness to it.

Derek: Sometimes when I meditate I feel something like that appearing but something in me still suppresses it.

Me: And see it in all its guises and how it tries to control you.

Derek: It's almost like I can feel it in my head.

Me: Then you will recognise it always and be able to call it out and laugh at it. Yes, once there is hyper awareness and acceptance of it, the power of it will dissipate.

Derek: Because I think it has faded away before.

Me: It will never leave you but the power dynamic shifts.

Derek: But when it comes to the surface I think I can think it into such a big thing when actually it's really nothing.

Almost feels like uncontrollably constant mental chatter which blinds me from reality.

Me: Yes it needs you to work on it.

Derek: I will reach out more.

Me: But great that you have some awareness around it. It means it's time to face it.

Derek: Worried it will kill me. Unleashing the beast. The worry is probably the main issue.

Me: Nah man, it won't if you do this work. So, research shadow work practitioners in the city, maybe look at if there is a ManKind Project initiation weekend. This shadow work will change everything man. It's more cosmic journeying. Really life-changing.

Derek: Sounds good! Tomorrow I will check it out properly!

Me: Yeh man, and in the meantime when you see your shadow rising to take control, see it, stare it out, observe it and realise it's just a part of you.

Derek: I just miss the time when I was a kid and I could just lay down and feel zero anxiety and just be present and so happy and alive and content. Now I feel like something in my mind rules me and blocks out pleasure.

Me: If you pause and just observe and ACCEPT that it is a part of you for a few mins, it may well start dissipating.

Derek: I will keep practising this man. Thank you for the support.

Me: Yeh man, pleasure. Like example... a voice saying 'go on do it...' if you just stop and examine what that voice is asking you and just kind of stare it out for a few mins you'll see it and its power will dissipate.

Derek: In my head though it's like it's out there to get me! Very OCD thoughts wanting me to be negative and to obsess. It's like if I tell myself not to think something then I will just keep thinking it.

Me: You're not telling yourself not to think something.

Derek: I don't think I can just stop.

Me: You are examining the voice. You need to examine what you are being told.

Derek: Consciously look at the voice?

Me: Yes, exactly, like a detective.

Derek: Like when you meditate and you watch your breath?

Me: Yes, consciously 'stare' the voice out, with love and acceptance for the voice, trying to understand it. Eventually you may get some awareness around where that voice originates from. You may not. But if you consciously stare it out for long enough it will lose its power.

Derek: And it won't make it stronger?

Me: No! That's the cosmic thing. As long as you don't try and change it.

Derek: OK. Thanks man.

Me: As long as you don't beat yourself up for thinking it.

Derek: Exactly.

Me: If you start saying 'why am I thinking this' it will grow.

Derek: Alright.

Me: When you stare at it you have to be non-judgemental.

Derek: Crazy minds.

Me: Be interested in it without judging it.

Derek: Befriend it?!

Me: Exactly, have compassion for it, Like 'hmmmmm... OK this is a very interesting thought, I wonder where you come from?'. Observing, non-judgemental. It is very important that you do not judge the thought.

Derek: I must sleep but let's talk soon man. I must practise to
    learn not to judge.
Me: Yes, just be interested in it! OK man sleep well. Observe
    well. Speak soon. Lots of love.

I know that being a musician is so hard, and there is a
lack of education in personal development and mindfulness
specific to a musician's lifestyle, not only about being able to
achieve your full potential, but dealing with the challenges
that life as a muso can bring.

If you understand the reasons why you are making
music, you will consider that what you are doing is absolutely
essential to the universe and that you must produce music
because you are the only
person in the world who
can say what you are saying
in the way you do and also
create the music that you do.
You will know that there is
nothing else at this moment
that you should be doing, or

> *to truly create from your heart, from your true self, you will need some tools and this book should provide them....*

into which you should be putting more effort. Only then will
you be successful and that is enough to carry you through.

Even more than that, in order to truly create from your
heart, from your true self, you will need some tools and this
book should provide them.

This section of the book is mainly about creating
awareness around the issues you face. This is the first step to
improvement. There are few solutions in this section (though
there are some); we will be looking at the solutions in much
greater detail in the following chapters, but it is important

that we firstly pinpoint where your pain, difficulties and challenges are coming from, in order to then be able to deal with them.

Anxiety:

Anxiety is not going to help you and it is not going to serve you. We will **learn how to put anxiety to the side and we will be able to shed your anxiety and clear the way for new thoughts.**

I only know about acute anxiety because I have definitely suffered from it in my time. I used a lot of drugs to try and distract myself from it and overcome it, but I realised that they just made things worse. At the height of my professional drumming career I would often use cannabis, LSD, Ecstasy, cigarettes, alcohol and various other drugs to escape my anxiety. Of course, this only made it worse in the end.

It meant that I was up much later than I needed to be. When I came home from a gig I would often smoke a large quantity of marijuana before I would eventually get to sleep – in the early hours, often as the sun was rising. On the days that I had to be at school where I worked as a drum teacher, I was off my head elsewhere and not on the job – although I enjoyed teaching. As a result, I am not sure how good I was at teaching, simply because my energy was not truthfully in it. I would bite my nails so much they hurt. I would worry constantly about whether I would ever make it as a professional musician and yet I *was* a professional musician, I was paying my rent and I was placing food on the table from the money I earned playing the drums.

How deluded we are when we don't realise what we have! So, my anxious energy was stopping me from moving forward in my life.

Don't fall victim to dreaming of better times, because when you look back, you may well realise that those times were great and that the only thing that was holding you back from fully enjoying and appreciating them was a dream of the future. The phrase 'it's about the journey not the destination' is truer than you may be willing to admit or understand. Is it possible that you can have in mind where it is that you are heading, without distracting from the here and now? There are bound to be unbelievable moments for you right now, those that you may never recreate due to your age or particular circumstances. Don't forgo the pleasure of those now because you are not where you want to be. What if you get there, and look back at the journey, and realise you missed some of the best times because you were sad that you hadn't arrived in the place which you were dreaming about.

Let's imagine an example; you are on a train journey with some friends to a festival. The chat is flowing, someone buys some drinks, but for some reason you just can't enjoy the journey. Whilst everyone else is in the moment, you are thinking about being at the festival. You get angry and frustrated at even having to travel to the festival thinking, *why can't we just be there already!* You spend so much energy on thinking about all of this that you really cause yourself so much distress during the journey that you arrive at the festival extremely agitated. It is only once you are finally starting to enjoy the festival that you look back on the journey and realise: 1. That it wasn't that bad; 2. That you made it much worse with your lack of acceptance of the facts and reality and; 3. Had you accepted the journey and been in the moment, you probably would have actually enjoyed it!

Having paranoid thoughts, lack of acceptance, lack of appreciation and GRATITUDE for all that I had, of the work that was needed and of looking for the good in the journey, would take over. The hours I would allow them to rule me would simply mean that I was not producing the kind of practice and clear subconscious flow that I needed in order to get to the next level. Therefore, the anxiety was actually creating inertia.

It's easy to feel that no one understands this, that no one goes through this like you do! No one is there to make/help you step up to the task, to make the changes that need to be made in order to climb to new levels. This can often be true and there is no easy way to say that it is unfortunately only up to us individually to make the necessary changes. You'll hear people tell you it is hard to change and, in a way, this is true. But also, in another way, it is not true because the truth is that if you start with only one action, this can easily lead to another action in the same direction (this is true for both negative and positive choices). Instead of focusing on the whole picture of where you need to be, focus on a small action that can be done now. By stepping up to that one small action, it can have a profound effect on your next move. A person gaining wisdom understands that if you do not make a change the same things happen; rather like the cliché of the madman who does the same thing over and over again expecting different results. The only way to make different results happen is to create change, and the only way we can create change is

> *you need to know that you will probably slip up − and that's OK − as long as you get up and try again...*

through our own motivation and making a clear decision as to what changes you can start with, putting them in a diary and sticking to them. All the time you need to know that you will probably slip up – and that's OK – as long as you get up and try again.

EXERCISE: Therefore, I encourage you, right now, to take a pen and paper and draw three columns. Write in the left-hand column: what you are not happy with in your life; in the middle column: the changes that would need to happen in order to create a different result; and in the right-hand column: the result you would like to happen as a creative being. I think it is well within your ability to make these changes happen and even, potentially, face them in an incredibly creative way. Put them up on your wall, somewhere visible where you will see them often; daily.

Stress also falls under the category of anxiety and can be caused by the feeling that you are not in control of your own existence. If you feel this regularly, then you are not taking control over your way of life.

Anxiety and stress are also caused by overthinking.

Alan Watts refers to overthinking in his lecture available online 'How to Stop Overthinking'. In it, he explains that the reason why we tend to overthink as humans is because, in our brains, we are able to anticipate oncoming dangers. We are able to perceive potential issues and dangers that may arise.

But, we tend to take this to a new level. Instead of only using our brains for potential dangers, we tend to overthink the dangers that may arise and even become part of creating new dangers by shaping our reality to include potential dangers that may not even happen.

The stress a musician experiences can come from many different angles. Drug use, alcohol abuse, smoking; these are all things that a musician will take to in order to distract themselves from the stress, except that all these things will contribute to more stress! As musicians we don't realise this. We think that having a toke on a cigarette, a spliff or a few drinks will make everything a bit better, because life is so difficult and it's a struggle. What you will find is that if the motivation for turning to these outlets is driven by escapist reasons, then they will not help in the long term, or even the next day, and you will find yourself impeded by the same worries and stress.

The problem is that we don't think about the next day and the knock-on effect; that by drinking too much tonight, how are we going to feel tomorrow? We forget about the fact that we are going to wake up a few hours later and never feel refreshed, ever, because of that hazy cannabis hangover. The fact is that when we take the MDMA after the big show, a few days later, we are going to think about all the reasons why our life is terrible, that we are never going to make it and that even the next gig is not going to be very good. As the book continues, we will be exploring ways to combat these patterns.

The feeling of a lack of control:
Continuing our discussion about stress, one of the symptoms is the feeling of a lack of control over our career. The feeling that we are waiting for the fans to buy music, we are waiting to create that new hit song, we are waiting for the booking agent to book the gigs or the guy in the band who is responsible

for booking the gigs. We are waiting for the artist to do the artwork, we are waiting to be able to afford to go into the studio to record the new track – and while we are waiting we feel out of control. The only time we feel like everything is moving well is when we go from rehearsal to gig, from gig to studio, from studio to holding the new product in our hands. If no one is showing us that they want to work with us in the business world and we feel that everything is failing and we are out of control, how are we ever going to make it? "I am waiting for the email from the big manager; I am waiting for the people to buy a record... Everything is out of control. I have no control over my career, I am just a musician who needs to create and that is all I can do."

This is the kind of attitude that leaves us feeling that our careers and lives are out of control. This kind of mindset will lead exactly to the path of destruction. It will lead to the path of no one really believing in you or your music. It will lead to inertia and nothing happening. Again, in this book, we will explore how to overcome this feeling.

External pressures:

This includes the 'financial pressures' part; working hard in a job to pay the bills and trying to deal with the music pressure from friends and family. I used to hate going to family events when I was drumming. The questions were generally: Brett, are you still drumming? How's that going? Do you actually make any money? How do you manage to do that? Where are you going with your life? Are you always going to be a drummer? Are you in a band? What's going on? So you play session gigs...? You teach? Oh good, but how often? How often do these session gigs come up? Etc., etc. I understand

> **I understand your struggles because I have been there too. I have been in those situations...**

this aspect well and it was most definitely awful!

This creates pressure from within yourself, you feel judged by others, then add in the dark feelings and the bad thoughts, and the result can be a low opinion of yourself that, on some days, can engulf and overwhelm you and make it feel impossible to even get out of bed. What they don't realise is that you NEED to do this. If you don't NEED to be an artist and you can think of other things that you would like to do as well, or even instead, then go do them!

Do you know the strongest way to combat these external pressures from people? Just be and talk your truth and even the uncle who's very judgemental will then respect you!

How would they react if you gave this kind of speech to those people by whom you feel judged?:

"Look, I chose a very hard path, but it's because I NEED to produce art. If I didn't I would die or be extremely/even more depressed. Unfortunately, this is the path I have chosen because I know my truth. I have to live on the edge, in the unknown and what looks like an unstable place, as that is the place from which the best art is created. I get lots of perks, and I will make enough money to live and get my pleasure from things other than money!"

What do you think a version of this (adapted for the person who is asking you these questions) would do? Well, it would shut them up, and it would make you stand tall and feel proud that you stood up for yourself!

Obviously, the highs come when you are actually playing a gig, with everyone smiling and dancing and singing, jumping up and down, or truly wrapped up and connected to you and your music. You've seen how it can be. You've seen friends' bands. Isn't that the worst – when you go to a gig of another band and they're doing much better than you and everything is going really well for them? – In fact you were nearly in that band and you turned it down because you wanted to write your own music. You wanted your own creative control – and now look at them! Look at that band! "They are doing much better than us!"

We must be pretty good when we play a gig. Everyone loves it – so why can't we be playing gigs every day? Why can't we live this life all the time? Why am I having to do another part-time job? Why am I not professional yet, and if I am professional, why is my career no better than it currently is?

THIS IS A VICTIM MENTALITY which will not help you succeed. The 'I should, I could, I would, Why not me?' attitude will not help you to succeed. I understand your struggles because I have been there too. I have been in those situations and I have fought my way through those circumstances and often still have to. I have worked with many professional musicians who have managed to overcome these situations too, and the one thing that links all the musicians who are successful, and have managed to break through, is that they have overcome this sense of victimhood. The ones who have managed to sustain long careers believe in something much bigger than themselves. They believe that they are only a part of the magic that has been created. They believe that they are able to tap into an energy that is unexplainable. They are able to bring their true creative flow from inside out and express themselves fully (speak their truth through music) with no blocks. In this book we are going to look at tangible techniques to help you to grow as a person, to overcome all of these challenges and to grow and express your creative truth.

This is not a book of fluff, nor is it about only highlighting all the problems, during the journey we are going to look at practical ways of overcoming the struggles, as we have already started touching on, and help you to live your truth proudly and with a smile on your face.

I heard a story of a wise man, he is a friend of a friend; an older guy, a wonderful man, a devout Buddhist and meditator, and he also teaches communication tools and techniques as a job to corporations and groups. He went on a 6-month (almost silent) Zone Technique retreat. My good friend asked him if he had taken away a simple learning or understanding from that experience. He thought about it and replied: "Conflict is inevitable."

Meaning that despite being surrounded by tranquility, and a few other meditators that were all focused on generating peace and goodwill, there were still conflicts that emerged either amongst the participants or within individuals. So, when I encounter any kind of disagreement, miscommunication or conflict, I try and remember that "conflict is inevitable"; it's no one's fault, no one is to blame, it was always going to happen. The reason for the richness of society is that we all have different life experiences and perspectives and so, conflict just has to be overcome. Therefore, I choose to embrace conflict and rise to the challenge, to think about the best approach to that conflict and to communicate as effectively as I can. We will be exploring these ideas deeply in the sections on Decision-Making and Conflict Resolution.

CHAPTER 2

Why The Zone Technique?

Attachment to certain things can be positive or negative. It is my belief that all things are neutral and it is up to us, as humans, to either put a positive or a negative spin on them. Try and think of anything where that is not true. Imagine, as humans we have the power to affect something positively or negatively. A well-known analogy is that a knife can be used for cutting and preparing a delicious dinner, or to injure someone; it is the human who decides. Maybe a less significant example is social media. It can be used to insult someone, or you can spread beautiful ideas. This is the same across new scientific discoveries and any object whatsoever.

A rarely known fact, that I mentioned earlier, is that accomplished musicians are successful meditators. As a musician, *you* are already a competent meditator. From the hours you have put in over the years, practising day in, day out, perfecting your craft, you have been entering that zone of subconscious flow; a timeless, weightless space. In this chapter I want to show you why this thing called 'Zone Technique' will be an incredibly useful part of your toolkit in accessing the zone. I will explain that by using the Zone Technique, you can get into that zone you are familiar with in minutes, without your instrument, away from the stage and without creating and *why* using this tool is *so* useful.

As we have said, entering the zone allows you to operate from your truth, reacting with your full being, through both your heart and mind. It is a place in which you are likely to find yourself after some time of playing, and it is the most useful and productive place for any artist to be. But you don't actually need to be creating, or using your instrument, to get to that same recognisable place, because your place in the zone is so established – there are other ways to get there.

Over many years, while I was a professional drummer and while I was a band manager, many of my friends would tell me about this thing called Zone Technique – how it helped them focus, stay grounded and find a little peace. My response was always "That's OK, I have music". However, I had received so many signs in my life about Zone Technique over the years. Quite a few friends had been on courses learning how to focus the mind. The techniques I am about to show you I learned on a 10-day course. We spent 10 days practising this technique, in utter silence, 12 hours a day! I now use this technique on a daily basis and it is like a magic trick. It can transport you to a peaceful place and completely calm the body and the mind.

A daily Zone Technique practice of just 10-20 minutes (I recommend morning and evening *and* stepping up the minutes once you get used to it) can provide you with a strong sense of happiness, acceptance, better judgement, appreciation for life and an ability to recognise your darkness and your light, and accept yourself as perfectly imperfect, as a being of light. No joke, this is *real*, it really is a magic wand. Yes, you have to be disciplined, but, really, it is the perfect solution for a happier life for certain. When you are craving and unhappy with where you are at, it can bring you back to a centre of peace inside yourself. It really does have these cosmic powers. On paper, you would never believe me, the only way to feel the benefits is by trying it.

I cast my mind back to the times that I was practising the same bar over and over again, how incredibly focused I was and how fulfilled I felt doing that (at times!). Well, that was the zone. The same zone I entered when in the rehearsal room or gig. But you know how frustrating it is trying to stay focused in practice. How common is it to lose concentration and slip up? Thoughts would enter my mind and drift me away from the practice. But the more I practised, the better I could enter that focused zone and eventually I could practise a bar over and over again at 45 bpm, for 45 minutes to an hour, and just get lost in it. Time would stop and I would be in a very deep, serene place. How skilled are you at practice now, because you have been doing it a long time? If you are not so skilled, you are getting better at maintaining that focus, aren't you? Well, this is the same process that meditators go through.

> *How common is it to lose concentration and slip up? Thoughts would enter my mind and drift me away from the practice...*

It is a tool that, in minutes, will help you drop into the zone. This is valuable because you no longer have to practise for ages to get there, you can get there in just a few minutes. So in preparing to practise or before a performance, you can begin playing, already in that zone.

Let's investigate the technique...

EXERCISE: First off, allocate some time. To start with in this investigation period, allocating 10 to 20 minutes will be ideal. (As you move forward you will increase the Zone Technique to 30 minute sessions.) Set an alarm (with a watch or phone – making sure the phone is on aeroplane mode!) so you're not distracted about how much time has passed.

Say to yourself – "I am dedicating these next 10-20 minutes to investigate Zone Technique and nothing else". That way, you'll know that when thoughts come into your mind to distract you, you can, with confidence, say to yourself "That thought is not what I'm doing now, that's for later, right now I'm using the Zone Technique".

So now you have reserved the time, close the door, put your phone on aeroplane mode and be alone. Enjoy the space and the fact you have given yourself this time just to enquire, to grow and to investigate.

Find a space to sit cross-legged. Use a pillow or two to sit on, making sure you're comfortable. To start with, this seating posture will be more sustainable if you use cushions to raise your bottom so that it's elevated higher than your knees; but whatever feels comfortable is fine. (I usually sit on my bed with a couple of cushions raising my bottom, but seating changes according to my location, which does not matter the more experienced you get.) If sitting cross-legged really doesn't work for you, sit on a chair with your feet on the ground, and not too slouched. It is just important not to lie down because this will induce sleep!

Next, close your eyes and start putting your attention on

to your breath, breathing in and out of your nose. Don't try to change or force the breath, just listen to it – is it a short or deep breath? Is it mostly in and out of the left or right nostril? The trick here is to be inquisitive. Become a detective investigating the nature of your breath, how it feels in your nostrils, how your chest rises and falls. This exploration and curiosity about your breath will really help you in the next part…

The nature of our minds is that they wander. We have trained our minds (or allowed them) to always think about something else. Usually this wandering takes the form of something that happened in the past ("I should have said something else" or "She should have not done that") or something that might happen in the future ("At 8 p.m. I must remember to…" or "Next Tuesday I'm going to go…"). But can you see how none of these thoughts help us in this present moment? The event that happened in the past has ended, it's over, and nothing can change that! The event that you're planning for the future may never take place, but if strong feelings of needing to plan come up, write some notes before you start. By making a note in the diary, or somewhere useful, it dumps the information out of your head and takes away the necessity of clinging on to these thoughts. The true reality is the present moment and the present task on which you have decided to focus.

So when a thought does come into your mind to distract you, just calmly say "That's for another time, it's not relevant to me now. Right now I'm focused on using the Zone Technique on my breath", and go back to focusing on your breath with inquisitiveness and curiosity. If your mind wanders after 10 seconds, don't get frustrated, just follow the technique, and eventually that 10 seconds will increase.

But remember, it is this practice of returning to your breath that is the foundation of your Zone Technique. The process of returning to the present moment, where your breath is waiting for you to investigate, is the

> **Become a detective investigating the nature of your breath, how it feels in your nostrils how your chest rises and falls...**

process of training your mind to be more present. If you do this for 10-20 minutes a day for 2 weeks, you will see a change in, the way your mind works, your interactions with other people and in your ability to drop into the zone.

Some people say at this point "I can't concentrate, there is too much noise in my head"!

If you are one of those people, I have two things to say to you:

1. That is exactly the process you must go through! It's like if you have to tidy the house but don't know where to start, or you want to write a song but don't know how to begin. You must begin and break through the noise.
2. Have the faith that this is only the very beginning and, of course, after a little practice you will improve and start to feel the benefits.

In order to clear the noise you must go through a process, it will not happen right away. Today you may hear noise the whole time, yet, you may find some stillness for 30 seconds. Next time the amount of noise will be slightly less. This may continue for some weeks. BUT it is worth sticking to, because I can tell you for sure, this technique works for all humans to clear our minds of clutter and noise.

Actually it's good that you can observe that there is a lot of noise and it proves that you need this more than anyone!

Taking the technique further

Still keep your focus on your breath, not trying to change it but just focusing on it. This is your anchor and you should feel a stability in being able to come back to the breath whenever you want – in any situation, at any time. It will always be there for you and will help you focus your mind, should you need to, even for half a minute.

Once you feel comfortable with this technique, I would suggest after 2 weeks of 10-20 minutes each day, we can start taking it further. Start your Zone Technique and whilst you're still focusing on your breath, and after a couple of minutes, start noticing how your body feels. Start at the top of your head and very slowly, scan each and every part of your body, feeling what you feel. Notice what sensations come up – you may feel cold, or itching, or heat, or a specific emotion in one part of your body. As you go through, don't move or try to change what's there, just notice, accept it and move on, with the understanding that this sensation has come, is going to stay for a very short amount of time, and then it inevitably will change in some way.

Slowly go through your body like this, scanning, breathing, not moving or trying to change anything. When your scanning arrives at your feet, start mentally moving back up your body again, from your toes to the top of your head. Then scan downwards from your head to your feet and so on. At any time, if you get distracted or find your mind in a different place, just come back to your breath and stay there until you feel that it's time to start again.

When you are scanning through your body, you might come across an area of tension or stress. At this point, just let your attention linger on this area. Don't try to change the nature of the sensation you find, just observe what you are feeling. Once again, start investigating it (like you have learnt to do with your breath). Be inquisitive; go into the sensation, even if it is painful. You will find that the more inquisitive you are, the easier it will be to deal with what you find. Whereas you might have previously classed this sensation as 'pain', now as you increase your inquisitiveness, you can observe it simply as just 'a sensation'. And when you're ready, move on to another part of your body, or go back to your breath.

Now you have this tool, keep practising every day. As you get to know it, you'll start using it to drop into the zone as you need to. For example, just before a practice you could spend 2 minutes in stillness, focused on your breath, noticing the sensations in your body. After 2 minutes you may be focused and aware enough to be in the zone and take it to your playing, or perhaps you could stay using the Zone Technique for a few minutes more until you drift further into the zone.

If you've been using the Zone Technique for a couple of weeks, but you're feeling a sense of frustration and nothing to do with what I have referred to as the zone, don't be disheartened. Just revise through the technique in this chapter and give it another week or two of using the Zone Technique every day. I would suggest that if you are using drugs and alcohol regularly, it will make it much harder to get into the

> **You will find that the more inquisitive you are, the easier it will be to deal with what you find...**

zone! At least if you're using the Zone Technique, you are practising strengthening and focusing your mind, however much you slip, lose concentration and feel distracted. As long as you keep focusing back on a sensation or your breath, without trying to change anything, then you will inevitably feel the benefits, like a calmness, stillness to the conscious mind that is normally noisy and an ability to tap into stressed areas of the body and feel the tightness dissipate as well as eventually recognising a connection to your zone.

I hold stress, anxiety and tension in the solar plexus (the pit of the stomach) and the front of my head (actually in the frontal lobe). Interestingly enough, when I observe the area at the front of my brain, which is the prefrontal cortex, without trying to change it, just observing, I can feel the tension releasing. This is so fascinating because it is this part of the brain which is considered by neuroscientists to be responsible for planning complex cognitive behaviour, personality expression, decision-making, and moderating social behaviour. The feeling of this area loosening and becoming relaxed is palpable for me, when I see these functions operating after a good session and for many, many hours afterwards. The solar plexus area is where I hold my anxiety and stress. Curiously, my family have a history of digestive issues and stomach problems, including hiatus hernias, and are susceptible to cancers in this area. Again, when I focus on this area and 'look and study' it while my eyes are shut but visualising the sensations and just observing, I feel the tension and anxiety releasing. When I feel anxious, angry, or frustrated now, I can check in with these areas and absolutely always realise that the tension in my body is sending messages to the brain to feel those difficult emotions.

I spend regular amounts of time every day checking in

with those areas. I find by using this Zone Technique, I can actually unblock these areas of tension!

CHECK IN WITH YOUR BREATHING
AS MUCH AS POSSIBLE:

When you feel worried and anxious during the day, check in with your breathing – check in with your breath for 5 minutes and you will realise you weren't breathing properly. When you feel angry, anxious or frustrated you will notice that you are not breathing regularly and you are tense in those areas, which you will become familiar with within your body, where you hold most tension...

Decide if you are trying to find a solution to this issue you are fretting about. How likely is it that you can fix this issue, or do you have to wait and see? If you think it is just worry then go back to your breath work.

How often can you remind yourself to observe your breath while doing other things?

The best habit-forming thing I have worked on most recently is EVERY time I feel stress or anxiety, I switch focus to observing my breathing and make sure I am breathing smoothly; then I relax and continue to observe my breathing. Once I have switched focus, I then scan the areas I know I feel stress in, as mentioned earlier, the solar plexus and head. I observe how tight they are. It normally turns out that the longer the time period that I have not checked in with my breathing and tension areas, the more tense and 'wound up' I am. If I have left it a day or so, I can really feel the tightness.

After years of practising, I can concentrate on other things whilst doing this; rather like the fact that you can play/sing music without consciously thinking about it.

GRATITUDE:

Expressing and feeling gratitude is one of the most important practices that you must make a part of your daily life. There are lots of ways in which you can do this; I recommend a classic tool that psychologists have been recommending for many years. Every evening before going to sleep, write a list of things that you are grateful for. At the beginning, to make it easy, you can start with only three. These can be as simple as 'I have a healthy body' (which, by the way, is *absolutely massive* and must be appreciated. Unfortunately, we often take this for granted and only realise when someone close to us no longer has good health, or if we ourselves suffer health issues). This should be done every evening before bed and every morning as you get up. Try and increase the list by one item every few days. Eventually, you will increase the list substantially. This exercise will gently train your mind to start focusing on positives. You should then use this as a springboard to thanking the universe out loud for those things for which you are grateful. If this practice is done regularly, you will notice it has a profound effect on your happiness levels. Through this process you will find that you are better at spotting the positive aspects of your life and reminding yourself of how blessed you are, even when things are tough and you are being challenged and pushed to your limit. This, along with Zone Technique, exercise, diet and creating, is one of the simplest, and yet most powerful, tools of change that you can practice.

EXISTENCE:

What do you think is the point to life? I believe that we are blessed souls, on earth to learn and grow, and that when we die it is not the end. In a later chapter I talk about mysticism and reincarnation and will deal with this in more detail, bottom line, I believe we are here to learn and grow and we will come back again. You don't need to agree. Viktor Frankl wrote in *Man's Search For Meaning* (Beacon Press, USA, 1959): 'Those who have a "why" to live, can bear with almost any "how"'. Meaning/purpose definitely help us to endure the challenges that life throws at us. What do you think you are doing here? If you can't come up with an answer, then you lack meaning. Without meaning, I am not sure there is a point to being here!

But, hold on, you are reading this book! Well, let's revisit 'the point'. How about the following: you have a skill and talent with music and you can make the world a better place by spreading joy through your art. It sounds like a good meaning and pursuit to me.

EXERCISE: Write your answers on a piece of paper to the following questions:

- What needs to happen to you, in order for you to be the strongest you can be?

- What do you have to do to make the best possible creations you are capable of?

- What are you learning in order to improve yourself?

- How are you developing yourself and what are you learning that can help others?

- What do you need to learn and do, so you can grow enough to be a positive light for others?

- In order to be a positive light, does it mean you need to move yourself into the light? How best can you do this right now?

- Who are you learning from, who inspires you to learn right now?

Look at the people you are learning from. Are they those who seem to be failures or those who seem to be successful? What is it that separates the two? Of course there is always room for improvement and there will always be mistakes, but are you learning from those and refining your practice all the time so that mistakes are fewer? Remember, all it takes is to make one positive change, one small thing that can fuel your movement towards another positive action.

CHAPTER 3

Honesty, Integrity and Not Hiding Your Truth

I hope you are not eating, as I have some graphic biology for you that won't last long, I promise!

In 2016 I was diagnosed as being infertile because my testicles were not performing properly. The reason for this was because, on reaching maturity, my scrotum remained too high in my body and failed to descend fully as normal. This resulted in my testicles being 'radiated', which means that my sperm died when I was in puberty. Furthermore, I was also informed that I still needed to have an operation to lower the testicles fully in order to avert the risk of testicular cancer.

This is obviously quite important and a potentially embarrassing story to tell people, but I was having a very serious operation and it was a part of what I was going through. I was looking at a 6-week recovery process and the surgeons were going to have to make four incisions above and below the actual area. After some consideration, I decided that I had to tell people. I wanted people to know because I was sick of the idea of having to skirt around the issue.

Of course, I was suffering anxious, nervous thoughts. I think that these could have been crushing to me had I not shared the embarrassing circumstances that were leading to major surgery. By the time I was heading for the operation, I had been using the Zone Technique for many years and had a strong daily practice. I was getting more in touch with understanding the sensations and the feeling of truth in my body, when thinking certain thoughts. I believe that I intrinsically recognised that I must speak out about this truth to people and share my anxieties and fears with others.

Instead of only telling one or two people though, I decided just to tell anyone when it came to expressing where I was at and what was going on in my life. I am not sure if there are many – if any – friends in my life right now, as I write this book, who don't know!

This experience had a profound effect on my attitude to telling people what we might consider a 'secret'.

As a result of sharing these intimate details about my life, especially to the ones who were not necessarily as close to me, it meant that they felt comfortable sharing intimate secrets about their existence and their life with me. Consequently, it has brought me closer together with many more people. I think, as humans, we crave truth and real connection. Through sharing our lives, it has made me a party to the idea that we all have our struggles; even people who appear to be very sorted can be facing incredible adversity. We all have huge challenges and we have all regularly experienced either shame, guilt or insecurity, perhaps all three!

> But if you knew what your colleague at work was going through... you would realise that you are not alone...

I argue that *no one* has an easy life, *everyone* has deep, deep challenges, whether you know about them or not. Just think about how powerful this personal sharing is from a trust perspective. In a way, you are communicating to someone "I trust you with my deepest, darkest secrets, which means that you can trust me with yours".

Only you know about *your* deepest challenges, *your* issues and *your* problems.

But if you knew what your colleague at work was going through, if you knew what your bandmate was going through or had experienced, you would realise that you are not alone.

Even though you *may* have these crazy, paranoid thoughts, this anxiety, this crushing voice that beats you up on a day-to-day basis and tells you that you are not doing well enough – it doesn't mean that other people don't. In fact, I would argue most people go through challenges that affect them similarly. They just don't tell you about all they've learnt and how to control those voices so that you can be the driver and not the passenger.

TELL PEOPLE YOUR DARKEST SECRETS, BE YOU, BE YOUR TRUTH, TELL AS MANY PEOPLE AS POSSIBLE WHAT'S WRONG WITH YOU. You can practise by just choosing to tell one person something you wouldn't normally tell anyone. Go on, just tell them; they will be honoured. I can almost assure you that as long as it is about you, and you are *not* going to violate them, then they will be honoured to hear your truth and will not judge you for it, rather they will respect you and look at you as brave, so tell them! (Tell them when you are sober, not when you are paralytic! You don't want to have to keep repeating yourself.) The caveat to this is that when you tell people, you must tell them with acceptance, not from a place of victimhood. "Why does this kind of thing happen to me?" or blaming someone else for your life situation (in other words having zero acceptance), will result in you sounding like a victim. If you speak about all the darkness that you are experiencing from a place of victimhood, then you will end up being the lonely, messed-up person in the corner of the party. But how wonderful it is that the only difference between that messed-up person and you is that you are willing to accept the unfortunate things that have happened. YOU OWN THEM.

If it was your error, you acknowledge the mistakes and are willing to learn from them and move on. If you really don't think it was you who acted badly, even after doing some serious soul-searching, then, with compassion, you can try and understand the reasons why someone else would behave in such a way. Can you think of times that you have acted in such a way? With enough work you can forgive the person. I am not suggesting this for any other reason than, if you can forgive someone then you can let anger go. When someone wrongs you, well, you have somehow allowed that to happen. What was your hand in that situation? How could you have behaved better, avoided the flare-up, or prevented the results happening that got you here? Unfortunately, there is no way any of us can get through life without someone cheating us, breaking our trust, or having to face adverse circumstances and situations. The best possible outcome of any painful scenario is that we look into ourselves and take responsibility, accepting our part in what happened. Of course, you can spend all day pointing out why the other person is to blame, but that will likely exacerbate and not cure the situation. If you recognise how you could be different and change, without beating yourself up, and with compassion, admit your wrongs and your flaws, then it lets the other person off the hook, and you will be able to let go and forgive easier. This also means you will be able to move on quicker and healthier. Not only that, you will learn and grow and head towards a place of not repeating unhelpful patterns that get you into trouble! Anger will only haunt you when you either, do not forgive yourself, or someone else, and do not let it go.

By owning your issues, you take away the other person's power. You take away the power behind feeling like you are hiding away from your truth and covering over the cracks. We all have cracks, and we all need to bare them. Once you have admitted your flaws, or the dark experiences, you retain your power.

The people who you know in your life who are always smiling; well, they have just learned to live with their shit. PLUS, how do you know they are always smiling?

I argue that you can open up about your difficulties, your life challenges. When someone asks you how the music is going, you can say "It's very, very, difficult. I've chosen a very difficult path. I have chosen this path because it is my truth and if I don't follow it I will be a very sad individual who is not living by the standards that I know I should be, BUT I know I CAN DO IT and I am really excited to achieve my goals!"

Don't be embarrassed about what you are doing. You are on a magnificent and noble path and I offer you tools in order to help you achieve your deepest

> **Once you have admitted your flaws, or the dark experiences, you retain your power...**

desires. These should not be desires of ego, but desires to fill people with your creation and expression, to help them; desires to make music, to be creative, to give that art to the world and to use your gift. You should celebrate your gift and you will learn how to control the paranoia and the anxiety, and face the challenges that your gift brings.

CHAPTER 4

The Practical Elements

I think we have now dealt with much of what might be called the 'spiritual' aspects and I have given you enough of the techniques to study. By practising daily, you will find they have a profound effect on your creative abilities. You will likely feel more connected to your creations, more focused, have better communication with bandmates and colleagues, and a heightened awareness, where everything flows better.

Now let's approach the sometimes chaotic way in which we rehearse, approach gigs and interact with the musicians around us.

The Sane Rehearsal:

Andy comes in from working in the flower shop for 8 hours. He's had a hectic day and is not very good at working at the flower shop, he just does it for money, and he doesn't enjoy it. He arrives and, being the band's drummer, starts setting up his kit. Everyone else is there and he goes on at everyone about what a rotten day he has had (even though he works in a flower shop; I mean, how bad can it be!).

Hopefully you are laughing a bit, but this scenario is instantly recognisable, isn't it? Andy is monopolising the conversation and the other members are thinking to themselves, *I also feel pretty crap today!*

Nicola, the singer, has been working in a school today and her head is very sore indeed, but Andy has been ruling the conversation. Then, in classic drummer style, what does he do as soon as he is set up? Yes! He sits behind the kit and starts banging his drums!

Well, if Jim, the bass player, wasn't already seething, he certainly is now – although Jim is a really placid kind of guy and is not going to say a word – but he is angry inside!

Patrick, the guitarist, is now really, really, pissed off, because he has been stacking shelves in Sainsbury's. Pat is a clever guy, with a degree, but he's doing it because, as it's shift work, it is a job that gives him flexibility so that he can accept gigs with the band.

Andy is ready to play now and everyone's rushing to get ready because they want him to stop playing drums. Someone shouts at Andy, "Can you stop playing the drums please mate?" He replies "yes" and he stops for one or two minutes, only to start tapping on the rims after a few minutes – as if that is less annoying! Well, slightly!

Everyone is getting a little bit frustrated and suddenly the only way to stop the noise is to join in and be part of it. So, noise begets noise and everyone starts jamming. There are a few smiles because you remember how much fun it is to play and people are thinking *actually this is quite a nice groove.* Either way, at some point, we have to interrupt this and make a plan for what we will be playing for the next several hours.

Where do you think all that frustration went? Do you think that entering the rehearsal in this way is the best possible way to start? Considering we've been talking about tension and areas of stress and anxiety, what do you think should have happened in that opening 20 minutes of set up time?

Once you have created in a mindful way and you have been using the Zone Technique, then you may well be taking your best material to the next rehearsal. There may be several writers in the band, maybe there is only one or even two. None of this matters.

What we are going to deal with here is how to set up a rehearsal, in a sane manner, so that everyone is on a level playing field in terms of their mood and approach to this rehearsal.

Do you think this set up helped towards reaching their full potential and getting all the creative juices flowing? Or rather, is there pent-up anxiety and stress that seems to have dissipated during the jam, but is still making people tense?

You're probably all pretty good musicians by now, you've played a lot and studied a lot, so you can get away with it, and you think you're doing OK but, actually, you are not hitting your potential. Let's look at an alternative model for running a rehearsal...

Everyone is just arriving into the rehearsal room. Everyone has had his or her difficult day. Dave sets up his drums and when he is finished he sits on the floor in front of his drum kit. YES!

How about a 'Rule 1'? Set up and sit away from your instrument! When everyone has finished setting up, they sit on the floor in a circle. Whoever is set up first gets to pick an object. In the middle of the circle – there may be a guitar pick, a drumstick, whatever it is. You are going to perform what is known as a 'check-in'. Someone takes the object and starts talking about their day, while everyone else remains quiet and attentive. Give each other around 3 to 5 minutes each.

Tell your bandmates:

How you feel right now.

(You can explain *why* to give a bit of context, but the emphasis has to be on *how you feel right now.*)

Concentrate on your feelings, because you are about to enter a zone of feelings, of freeing up the conscious mind and unlocking the flow in the subconscious mind.

A healthy check-in would look like this:

Chris's check-in:

"Hey guys, I am worried about money, my girlfriend left again a few days ago… I am sad and it is affecting me right now. I am obviously worried about lots of expenses I have and what is going to happen with my living space, so I am quite agitated and upset. That's where I am at. I would love to chat to you guys more about it in the pub after the session."

Notice in the example above that the emphasis is on *where things are at right now* and that the reasons are relevant, but they are not the emphasis. The suggestion that Chris would really like to chat about this later, in more detail, is a great invite and if people can, then it will only help bring everyone closer together. After all, Chris has agreed to be open with his feelings and is inviting everyone in, which means he values and respects them all, which is a real compliment. The act of everyone listening to Chris, and offering him support, is a massive help to him and will only bring the group closer together. But, in the meantime, there is the work of rehearsing to do, and therefore it is not appropriate to go into Chris's story right now. But everyone should acknowledge him and, if appropriate, arrange another time to speak about his important and troubling situation.

When a person has finished speaking, it is very important that you all have a phrase where you acknowledge that you have heard what that person was saying. It can be as simple as, "I have heard you", or one word, whatever you guys feel would be a suitable word for communicating that you have heard your bandmate.

For respect and equality, there should be complete silence when anyone is sharing, you can nod of course, you can express agreement by waving hands, but no talking at all, this space is a sacred space for the person who is expressing themselves at that moment.

The biggest reason for this is to confirm that people are being witnessed and heard. When I am witnessed and heard a lot of the stress goes away, because I feel like I am no longer carrying all that weight by myself and I am understood. This is more important than remembering what everyone said. It is most important to empathise with people in the moment.

So you've decided on a phrase, you've said the phrase at the end of the sharing, and then you move on to the next person (the object is passed to the next person who is going to share). When you've all finished, just look at each other and appreciate your band family. Appreciate where you are all at and take some deep breaths together. As humans you should appreciate where you're at. You are a family. You are a family structure, maybe less dysfunctional than your family!

Or, perhaps more dysfunctional – maybe that's where the magic comes from.

So now you all have a good idea of how people are feeling, how their day was, and you have brought some empathy and understanding into the room. The next thing to do is to go around the circle again and express your intentions for this rehearsal. Perhaps it is a new song you've written that you want to bring to the band, perhaps you've got a gig coming up and one of you feels like you need to practise certain songs more than other songs. Pass the object, again no one else talks, everyone listens intently. When you have heard, say the word/phrase and move to the next person.

It goes without saying, do not take 20 minutes each otherwise you will ruin your rehearsal time. Try to be concise!

Each of you might come up with a different opinion of how to use the time. It is very important for everyone that there is no talking when someone expresses what they would like to work on. Allow each person to say the phrases below and acknowledge each answer.

"I would like to work on… today, because I think…"

Once you've gone around the circle and heard each other, perhaps there were some giggles because one person's answer was more predictable than another's – for example, you know that Patrick always wants to work on the endings because he's got a thing about endings – OK, so laugh about it, enjoy yourself. You then need to discuss everyone's points. It's very important that you hear each other out during that discussion. It needs to be a fluid dialogue, where there is space and no one individual dominates it. Between you, there should be a consensus that you are managing to make everyone happy and that you are covering most of what people wanted, bearing in mind urgency and necessity. In a later chapter, I discuss consensus decision-making verses majority decision-making. It will be useful to read that and use it in this situation, if necessary.

During this discussion and during the entire rehearsal, remember where your friends have come from that day. Remember what they said in their 'check-in'. It is very important that you relate to these people on a decent level, on a human level, where you understand and you empathise with your fellow musician, your fellow bandmates, your family.

Just before you are about to rehearse, I want you to do a shortened version of the Zone Technique. If it's a bit too intense sitting in a circle you can find a different space in the rehearsal room, no problem. Someone set the timer on their phone for five minutes, then just breathe and allow conscious thought to dissipate, allowing in the space. When the alarm goes off you end by acknowledging each other, smiling with an 'OK, let's get on with creating' feeling in the room!

I think that is going to make a huge difference to the way you rehearse; the improved productivity, the better feelings about rehearsing, the more positive feelings toward your bandmates and so much more. You can now feel connected, free of conflict and full of understanding for each other, with focus for the work in hand and fully able to relax and enjoy the groove.

Enjoy your rehearsals from now on knowing you are being held within a system that recognises you,

> " *If it's a bit too intense sitting in a circle you can find a different space in the rehearsal room, no problem....*

your daily struggles, and which enables you to feel the love from your fellow bandmates.

The Sane Gig:

So, much like the rehearsal situation, let's put in place some techniques to handle the gig situation.

Of course, once again, you've arrived at the venue. It is messy; there are other bands playing and sound checking, it's all very noisy and (unless you are blessed with roadies) you've got to do the unloading – it's all very hectic! So, I would suggest that there needs to be a few minutes of Zone Technique before the soundcheck, if possible, as a group; when you've all turned up at the venue, when you are all there and you've spoken to the sound engineer/venue manager/ promoter/artist liaison/your management, whoever is there to direct and help you.

You know when you are due to soundcheck. So, here is the calculation on your part: is there time for a check-in and Zone Technique before the soundcheck? If you are going to be waiting around for hours then I would advise that you find a quiet spot and do your check-in like you do in rehearsal. Instead of the 'what are we working on?' section, you will instead do a 'what shall we soundcheck?'. If there is not enough time, then you'll have to do it all later. There is no problem doing the check-in and intentions section and then using the Zone Technique later.

It would be interesting to consider inviting the other bands to join you, whether they have read this book or not. These are easy concepts to implement with others. Firstly, be natural and invite them, maybe one of you comes across much friendlier than another. You should suggest that the 'friendly' one invites the other bands. But, don't get attached to the outcome. If the other bands refuse, then leave it and DON'T JUDGE THEM. We don't want to destroy building a good atmosphere for the night. But imagine if they do join and the profound effect on the evening. The atmosphere between all the bands affects the audience, who will feel it, but perhaps won't know exactly why the night feels different. The audience will feel something cosmic through connection. Imagine the power of the check-in, the intentions for the night and the mini Zone Technique with all the other bands? Now you can think kind and good thoughts about those other bands, instead of feeling jealousy, or loathing, for the other band/s.

I remember when touring in Japan with a band I managed for many years, we were the support act, but we all got on very well with the main act and on the final gig, the headliners invited our lot on to the stage. They did a cover of the Velvet Underground's 'White Light/White Heat'. It was a fantastic spectacle, our drummer got on stage and their drummer, who was already playing the intro groove, started getting up, they managed to swap whilst keeping a beat going. Their drummer went to the front and started sharing the lead vocal mic to sing backing vocals. Our lead singer was playing harmonica and our bass player was just jumping around and singing a bit. The audience went up a gear in reaction and the whole place felt absolutely electric. Like everyone in the venue was connected. We all absolutely loved it.

A gig scenario can be very hectic and, by contrast, there can also be a lot of waiting around. To do the Zone Technique and check-in can bring you all closer in a profound way. Of course, it is quite odd to welcome another band to join you

> *whatever you do, in terms of the toxins, will affect you for some time to come, particularly the next day.*

in this way. You may feel like they will brand you as 'weird hippies'. Well, who really cares? Firstly, it is worth saying at this point that confidence in yourself and your beliefs is a huge thing! The trick is to stand your ground and believe 100% in what you are doing. If you do, and are willing to calmly challenge opposing views, you'll be surprised by how prepared people are to accept your point of view or at least understand you better.

If you understand why you use the Zone Technique and are able to convey these thoughts to the other band, then that will help. Acknowledge that it is a bit 'way out' but, then again, so is getting on stage and playing a bunch of songs you have written about all manner of personal stuff! As a result of practising the Zone Technique, both on your own and as a band, you have a story to tell about how it has positively impacted on your lives. You can speak about the fact that it will completely destroy any weird preconceptions, prejudgements and rivalries you may have between each other, and will bring you all together to create a profound atmosphere for the audience. Lastly, you can talk about 'the zone' that they obviously know, love and recognise. You can explain how it will also calm nerves, make everyone much more relaxed, and connect you to each other, the music and what you are all going to create on that night. It will ground you, make you more present and more able to connect to each other and the audience.

Whatever happens, you will need to find somewhere

quiet, even if it is the restaurant in which you are eating or somewhere you've gone to chill out, perhaps the dressing room, depending on whether other bands are sound checking.

You know, if you are using the Zone Technique with another band, don't be shy to limit it to 15-20 minutes, just for convenience. Also, 15-20 minutes of really allowing yourself to get deep is better than doing half an hour and still worrying whether you are needed to soundcheck or set up. One of you may wish to lead the Zone Technique for the first few minutes, just using some of the explanations I used in Chapter 2, to help people get into the zone, and it may help those who have not really practised before, though it is not essential.

You can also be open and truthful with the promoter or sound engineer, basically anyone who is likely to disturb you. Let them know not to disturb you, that you are all going to be using the Zone Technique until some set time.

We will be covering drink and drugs later, but may I suggest to you that you are strict with yourself and do not indulge in more than a pint or two of beer, a glass of wine or a light spliff before you play.

I have done it. We've all done it. If you ask yourself, honestly, was that gig any better after drinking three pints, after you did half a pill, or after a couple of lines of coke, really? Was it really better or was that just your perception?

If you recorded the gig, I would suggest that you've already heard that it was not good, it was not your best and not what you are capable of.

Of course, drink afterwards. Just know that whatever you do, in terms of the toxins, will affect you for some time to come, particularly the next day. We will come to this later because I have much to say on the subject of drugs, having done a lot myself!

As an aside, there is some logistical and practical advice when dealing with a sound engineer in a soundcheck... The next two paragraphs are relevant if you do not have your own sound man or manager/tour manager.

My suggestion is to select one member of the band to lead the soundcheck – this is incredibly important. In order to run that gig properly, you should have one member of the band who liaises with the sound engineer. This person is like a conductor, he checks with the sound engineer what is wanted next. Say, for example, the sound engineer says; "Drums" through the foldback mic, the elected 'sound checker' questions "all drums or just bass drum or snare?". The engineer comes back and says "Bass drum only first" and then the 'soundcheck conductor' as we can call them, signals to the drummer 'bass drum'. Repeat this system for all the instruments. Of course, if each musician can hear the sound engineer there is no need to keep repeating what they are saying! Just make sure that the 'soundcheck conductor' is helping make sure the next person is ready and is responding to the sound engineer, whilst no one else is interrupting at all. Basically, you will transform your relationship with any sound man by being as slick and easy to work with as this!

You should use the same approach for whoever deals with the promoter, regarding money or questions. When you first turn up, explain who you are, your name, what you do in the band and tell them you are the rep for the band in terms of money, riders, mealtimes and orders. You should make sure that you ask everyone in the band all the right questions and communicate back to the promoter at the relevant time. It is worthwhile, right at the beginning, to ask how the promoter likes to work in all these areas and how you can best assist them with getting all these items sorted, with the least stress possible, for the venue.

All of this contributes to people enjoying working with you. One of the key ways of generating your own success is by being liked. You really should not underestimate the power of people in the industry saying: "They were a really, really, nice bunch!"

JUST BEFORE GOING ON STAGE:

Before playing the show, you should form a circle and appoint one person as leader for this. Maybe it's someone who didn't do it last time, or someone who feels they have stuff to say. You should lead everyone into a sacred space. Two things should be included in this space...

- **Gratitude:**

Thank whatever spiritual force you believe exists, be it: God, the universe, sacred powers, universal energy, or even your bandmates. Make sure you all join in thanks for being able to write, create music and perform it to an audience. If there are not many people at the show, have gratitude for the ones who are. How often do you get to perform to any number of people... INCLUDING YOUR BANDMATES?

As a side note, if you feel the numbers are lacking, make a pact that, for that night, you are playing for each other. You are there for each other and you will enjoy everyone's performance.

- **Intentions:**

This is where you can state intentions for the show. These can be any intentions, be as creative as you like, but be relevant.

Nervousness and anxiety on stage while you are playing:

If you are anxious, thoughts can present themselves while you are actually playing the gig. Sometimes, if you feed them, they can be absolutely overpowering. In my early days of drumming and playing gigs – when I was not 'seasoned' – I would make an enormous mess, or certainly what I thought was a mess.

As a drummer, to stop playing during a piece of music LIVE is a faux pas of the highest order, unless the notes played next make it look planned. When I was in my early twenties, I remember that I was playing a session gig – I was standing in for a great technical drummer who had years on me in terms of his ability and knowledge. We were playing a couple of gigs; one was at the Hull Truck Theatre... I was playing difficult grooves, which I had not properly learned. It became apparent to me that I really had not nailed it, and I had myself tied in knots trying to play this groove in time and correctly. We reached the point where, I think I was even out of time, I had gone red in the face and actually had to stop. It was an awful moment and one that I never replicated in my career ever again. I learned a lot from that gig and I started inventing ways of managing my head when playing live.

To avoid this kind of situation, of course, you need to rehearse and you need to know what you're playing live, back to front and upside down. You've heard this all before and I am not here to lecture you on these matters.

Sometimes, however, you feel that you're fine with the music – let's assume that you are good with it all. You have played it many, many times and there is no reason why you should mess it up, but because you feed your

> **I would often watch the bass player...really focusing on their fingers and zoning in on the sound being produced....**

mind, your conscious mind is telling you that you haven't got it nailed; you are not sure because you can't hear properly, the monitors are crackling and you need to hear better, there is a cue line for the vocals coming up (or perhaps *is it twice around at the end, or 3 times?*), you can't hear the bass, and you are meant to play an intricate line with… etc., etc. So, we need to grab control of the mind, very quickly, and make sure that we have some techniques to bring us back to the music.

One technique that I use a lot is focusing on your hands, the hands that are actually playing the instrument. Whatever instrument you play, you can simply look at your hands playing the instrument, observe them, study them and this should bring your mind back to focus. It is an excellent way of bringing quiet to the mind and bringing you back to what you're playing.

Another really good way is to focus your mind on someone else's playing, or on your own SOUND, so that you focus on what you're hearing – really focus on whichever instrument you are playing closest to. Your favourite sound may be in that track, the bassline, or the keys line, or the vocal, or your own and so on. I would often watch the bass player playing, really focusing on their fingers and zoning in on the sound being produced. This would always help quieten my mind immediately. If you are the vocalist, try and focus on the tones coming out of your mouth or the sensations in your neck around your vocal cords, that can help you to keep your singing strong and in tune. Also try to focus on whatever is really giving you a foundation. Maybe it's the keys, maybe it's the bass, maybe it's the guitar and you need to focus on that. Maybe you love the rhythm of the drums, that's great as well, so focusing on those is fine too.

And don't forget to BREATHE, this is also very important! If you feel negative or anxious thoughts entering your mind, take some deep breaths and then focus on one of those aspects, either the listening or looking at your limbs. These things will really help your mind, it will bring you back, I promise. If you follow these techniques, you'll come right back to the present, so try these out in rehearsal and you'll really feel that the focus is coming through in these techniques.

Sane Recording – studio time:

I remember seeing an interview with Michael Jackson about Quincy Jones who produced the *Off The Wall, Thriller* and *Bad* albums. He was saying that Quincy would make him do takes over and over again. Then just when he thought he had finished Quincy would say "that is perfect, Michael! Do you think you can just do ONE more?".

You can take the approach of doing takes over and over again. I think we are living in different times now and, speaking from experience of playing and being in the studio with a lot of artists, Quincy's approach would not necessarily work with a band nowadays. In my experience the first few takes are the best, as you tend not to overthink your performance and come in with a fresh mind and space in your head to focus fully. It's bound to be more natural and have an exciting, fresh vibe. However, the decision is not mine, and if you strongly disagree then you do what you feel is best (and I'm not saying that like an annoying parent says it, to imbue you with a feeling of guilt!).

I really want to look at the whole process of making an album and bring all of the practices from previous chapters into making the album, or the single, or whatever recording you are embarking on.

I would suggest that 2 weeks before you go into the studio to record, you earmark these weeks for pre-production sessions. This is essentially rehearsing for 2 weeks before you go into the studio. Perhaps you'll invite the engineer and producer from the studio down to some of the sessions. Perhaps you're going to record some of the sessions and towards the end, invite some of the session players down, who will appear on the recording, to practise their parts with you. Perhaps you will practise just the bass player and drummer for a bit and then the other instruments against each other. Think about overdub lines that you will be using. Each person should take responsibility for each overdub line they will be playing. You should record these sessions, study them every night and discuss them the next day before starting the new practice session.

Recording is a big commitment and it is essential that you arrive with a good attitude. This is the perfect time to practise by making sure you do the 'check-in' every morning, speak about intentions and use the Zone Technique. This will be at both the pre-production sessions and in the studio. You should explain to whoever you are

> *...you need to be in a mindset where you nail those first few takes of each song...*

recording with that, once set up, you need 30 minutes to go through some rituals that help you be more productive and create a better atmosphere in the studio. These are the same 'new rituals' that you will go through at rehearsals, those that we recently discussed: Zone Technique, check-ins and intentions for that day's session.

The intention of this 2-week period is that you will be able to decide on final musical arrangements for each track and which overdubs you deem to be necessary. Of course, new ideas will come when you are in the studio and you may drop some of your earlier ideas, but you need to take in ideas with you so that you are not wasting valuable time and money when you are in the recording studio.

The other reason why you're doing this is because you need to be in a mindset where you nail those first few takes of each song. You don't want to be going into the studio with the potential stress of not nailing your parts.

Your first take, your second take and your third take are the ones with little or no pressure. Once you pass take number three, you may be starting to wonder how long you'll be doing this for! If you do pass take number three and it's not satisfactory, check in with your body, those tension areas, and if you feel like you are getting wound up it is worth stopping – sit and use the Zone Technique for a comfortable amount of time, thereby clearing the mind and allowing negative thoughts to dissipate and tension areas to loosen. You need to offer each other affirmations, smiles and laughter, and know that together, you will nail this and it's going to be fine. Also, remember the techniques that we recently looked at for live playing and focusing your mind. If you feel the pressure of the negative voices, then use those techniques as well.

Hopefully, after 2 weeks of pre-production sessions, you are ready to take the studio by storm.

Whoever you're working with in the studio environment, whether it's a new person or a friend, I suggest you introduce them to the new techniques you've been using and invite them into the circle. Introduce them to the framework you now use to set up rehearsals, gigs and studio time. On the first morning, and every morning after that, you are going to do your 'check-in'. You're going to set your intentions for the day and you are going to do a Zone Technique practice together with the producer and engineer, in fact anyone who is in the studio, be it an assistant or anyone else, it's a shared space of creativity. It's going to be your space for that day/week/month and whoever is there has an influence over the atmosphere, that's why you should include them in your work to make it what we will call a 'heart space', a feeling of true expression and creativity, love and openness.

We covered this next point just prior to the pre-production work but let's now review what you need to be doing; just remember to breathe! If you do end up making more than three takes, if anyone feels that they're losing it a bit and the conscious mind is chattering too much, causing anxiety to build up, then one of you should have the strength and vision to call time out. Call a 5-10-minute break – you don't all have to start sitting in a circle. If you are in a vocal booth or drum booth, then just sit and do some breathing and Zone Technique in there. You will bring some spiritual vibes to the space, some 'other' to it.

Start doing Zone Technique and start unblocking; just say to everyone, "guys I need 5 minutes out". You know that if you take 5 minutes or 10 minutes out of the day you will probably gain hours of productivity. It may feel counter-intuitive, but if you don't, you could end up trying to record three, four or even more takes whilst getting increasingly frustrated. Then someone loses the plot and you decide to go and get a sandwich. That half-hour break is much longer than the 10 minutes it would have taken to quietly use the Zone Technique, and who says that going for a sandwich/cigarette/beer is going to shift any blockage OR prepare you better for the hours of recording and concentration you still have ahead of you?

ZONE TECHNIQUE REMINDER:

- **Sit comfortably and close your eyes**
- **Concentrate on one thing only – Observe Breath or Visualising/Observing an area of the body**
- **Do not try to change it, just observe it without doing anything**
- **Check that your breathing is regular and deep**
- **Continue this for 10-20 mins**

Remember how great the Zone Technique can be, it can really shift everything, take you out of your head and show you other realms, pushing you on to a peaceful and creative plane.

So don't think that you haven't got time. I have often argued with myself that I don't have time to use the Zone Technique and, lo and behold, the day becomes even messier, things go wrong, time is wasted and I think to myself; if only I had taken that 20-30 minutes at the beginning of the day! Inevitably, I end up taking that time at a later point and then things start falling into place.

The thinking behind this is that panic, anxiety and stress are sure-fire ways of creating even more panic, anxiety and stress. They feed themselves because you are operating from a low mood point and you are in a bad way. How often do you start cracking jokes, seeing the funny side and belly laughing from an angry place? It is rare, unless you are extremely good at dry humour! If you are angry, you are shouting and you want to throw things, how

> *... don't think you haven't got time...I have often argued with myself that I don't have time to meditate...*

often do you end up becoming even more infuriated before someone steps in and says you are getting too enraged and out of control? This scenario is probably much more likely than you starting to crack jokes after shouting and losing it! So remember to take the time to use the Zone Technique and ensure you have the right mindset.

And there's so much more to say about the recording process...

Firstly, trust the producer/engineer you work with because they have an outside view. They are not stuck in your bubble of thinking everything you do is great. When they say enough is enough, perhaps it is worth trusting them!

When is a piece of art finished? When you decide to STOP! Once you stop and take a decision that nothing else will be added, played with, manipulated, mixed or mastered, it is officially finished. One of the finest jobs of a producer is to respond to band members who want to add more, by strictly saying: "NO MORE! It is done!"

If you are checking in every day, sharing your intentions and using the Zone Technique every morning. If you are doing long days, I would suggest that you sit and do another session at about 3 o'clock in the afternoon. Try and push your finishing times 30-45 minutes over your standard times to make the space for your new system of check-ins and Zone Technique – explaining to the people you are working with that this time is needed and why it is useful.

Now this is something to fall back on at any time: the studio gets mega stressed, you get into a rut and you are feeling bad vibes from people. You need to explain that Zone Technique is not going to happen every 10 minutes (over and above your short morning and afternoon sessions), but you want anyone in the studio to be aware that there is a possibility that you may take short breaks to recalibrate, and just sit and breathe for five minutes, before returning to the music. It's effectively no different from people calling ciggy breaks, which you may wish to replace with Zone Technique! A mini Zone Technique sit can be highly beneficial when things get too intense.

I was at a friend's recently for a dinner party, it was

buffet-style and so we were all standing picking at the food on the table. There was music playing at a reasonable volume. As I was the designated 'DJ' and had the ability to subtly manipulate the volume from my phone, I started turning the music up a bit. The energy in the room started rising and after several minutes a wine glass was accidentally smashed. At the end of the night when everyone had left (I was staying over), we started discussing the evening and the various conversations and things that had happened. My friend remarked that he had predicted in his head that something was going to get broken at that moment. He explained that he had felt the energy of the room rising and rising, the atmosphere getting more and more raucous, and it would not stop rising until a point when someone, who was having a little dance, swung around and accidentally swept a wine glass off the table. We then discussed other examples of this happening. What was most interesting about his analysis was the idea that once the glass had been smashed, there was a clear break in the atmosphere. It was almost like a line in the sand, a complete break from what had gone before, and after the initial 30 seconds to a minute of dealing with the glass, we created an entirely different vibe. I can also see this in visualising how fights break out, there is a rise in tension, anger builds and builds, it is palpable in the air when someone is about to throw a punch!

What we often end up doing is getting caught in a mood, which accelerates and snowballs. Stopping and using the Zone Technique for 10 minutes reverses your frustration and helps create some space between the old and the new mood. The Zone Technique will give you a period of reflection and time to breathe, unblock some stress and remember that generally everything is great. Remember – you're in the studio making a record, how great is that!

To give you another 'for instance' about how this works out, I can tell you that at this very moment of writing, I have been anxious all day. This is because while I have been working all day with musicians in my management/ coaching role, I have, at the same time, been preoccupied with thoughts of; *I really need to finish this chapter*. I need to get the book out there because I know this material is going to be really useful. Having taught many of these concepts on an individual basis, this book is now going to be referred to by more people and will, hopefully, have a positive impact on their lives. It can change the creative process for the better and make everything easier for the pro, or aspiring pro, musician. I, therefore, went to the gym, used the Zone Technique, to put some space between the anxious feeling and the writing. As a result, I have returned capable of completing this chapter. When I lose the plot again (which I know I will), I will probably sit and use the Zone Technique for 10 to 20 minutes just to recalibrate.

CHAPTER 5

Past Destructions

If I could see any act again and again, it would be Stevie Wonder. I have been so fortunate to see him twice live in the same summer. Once at Glastonbury Festival's 40th birthday; he was the closing act on Sunday evening on the Pyramid Stage and it was surely one of the finest gigs I have ever been to. Then, I was able to see him again in the August of that same summer, when I was tour managing one of the bands I managed who were playing Summer Sonic Festival in Japan. We were free to go and see him, and I went with a load of Japanese friends who were hungry. I went backstage to find some food and, until I was caught red-handed, I didn't realise that I was actually stealing food from Stevie's rider! A sweet Japanese girl came to me saying, "You Stevie's people?" I embarrassingly responded "Yes". As I was saying that his limo was pulling up! I took the load of sandwiches (ALL sandwiches in Japan have their crust removed, it is quite something!), snacks and drinks and scarpered, as he was getting out the limo.

Of course I was a hero to my friends, who were out front, bringing a load of refreshments and booze! My excuse for this was that Stevie Wonder, of all people, could order more, but it was pretty unprofessional behaviour and I was young and out of order at that age. I recently had a proper go at a band for stealing another band's rider at a festival show, albeit the show was minute compared to the Stevie festival show. It's a story, though, which I enjoy telling from time to time, just to give an example of my low-level behaviour, to which I must admit, along with the hypocrisy! I don't want to be one of those teachers that pretends I am super human and never do anything wrong. In fact, I submit to needing to re-read this book as much as anyone else.

The point of this chapter is to lay out some of the destructive behaviour that I have come across or have even performed myself. Some of it was my own, as a manager or band member, and some of it was caused by other band members.

I am going to cite examples of things that happened during my musical career that I believe were completely avoidable and had a great impact on those bands. This means that they could no longer operate as well as they had been, inevitably meaning that momentum was shot and morale diminished.

Hopefully, these examples are shared as a warning of what can go wrong and may also help you to isolate the warning signs in a band, or other situations, in which you are involved.

One of the first bands I was involved with that had promise, and they could have, I believe, 'made it', for want of a better phrase, was a live dance music project.

The band had two main songwriters. We were a completely live dance music act that had the energy of 70s Led Zeppelin-style rock and beats inspired by drum and bass, but played on my acoustic drum kit. It was around the time of Roni Size's incredible album *New Forms*, so it was the season to be making live dance music – but there were not many projects in the public eye or with records out. In the year 2000 we had recorded music, we had gigs under our belt and had even won the Leeds Battle of the Bands Competition beating a band by the name of 'Parva' (the same band and line-up that went on to be called the 'Kaiser Chiefs' and you know the rest!). As I said, we had a more rock 'n' roll, Led Zeppelin approach to the dance music scene and mixed double bass, decks, distorted, flanged and 'wah-wah' guitars, vocal, percussion and keyboards to bring a very powerful, melodic, electronica-influenced, original sound. We were all pretty accomplished musicians – we partied, took drugs, played music and lived quite the rock 'n' roll life around Leeds for several years.

I actually had a band rehearsal room in my bedroom. In addition to my own drum kit, the decks were set up, plus the guitar amps and the bass amp, which were all permanently there. I lived with six medical students and a sports science student, who never minded us playing music, day or night, which was amazing of them, seeing as they all managed to get good degrees and are all successful today.

We were medium-sized fish in a small pond, but we thought and acted like we were rock stars. We had access to very good-quality drugs, at very cheap prices, because we knew people and we took full advantage of that. We were also fortunate

> **...we had gigs under our belt and had even won the Leeds Battle of the Bands Competition...**

enough to be living at a time when pints were £1.50 in our local pub, cigarettes were cheap and we had a very good life for the 3/4 years we were together.

The guitarist and the keyboard player were extremely volatile people and, though we are good friends today and I love them dearly, they were completely infuriating. They had different styles and tastes in music, and they had very different opinions about every tune and where to take it. When they could agree there would be genius present; they were both extremely creative and had loads of ideas. But communication was an issue and rehearsals would often descend into arguments, and eventually there was nowhere to go except to the pub because these guys couldn't get on any more! The rehearsal would be ruined because someone would throw a tantrum and it would be difficult to turn things around.

Early on, people started offering to help the band. We had loads of, what I call, 'blokes in a pub' giving advice about direction and ideas. We were all easily swayed, in various directions, depending on who was telling us what. Ultimately, we were not centred. We were up and down in ourselves, none of us were entirely happy with our own existences. We were volatile people, so, knee-jerk reactions and quick decisions were made. A friend of ours, who was far more sensible and wiser than us, offered to manage us (he was also a student and his brother was in the band, he could obviously see the potential). He is now a producer in BBC Radio and has forged a successful career in the entertainment world. We took him on board and then not long afterwards we sacked him. I sacked him, not because I wanted to, but because everyone egged me on and silly old me went with the energy.

So I fired him for no good reason. We got a singer at the drop of a hat, then we fired her, then we got another singer. We were terrible at making decisions and we allowed ourselves to be guided by whims, whichever way the wind was blowing, whatever we were feeling, going with the loudest voice of the moment, eventually driving ourselves to destruction. I realise that many of these decisions were made on comedowns, in between big nights. So, on drunken/drugged up nights, we were making decisions that would have a huge impact on the lifespan of the band. Not a good idea!

This is an example of an extremely talented band, who knew we had what it would take musically and conceptually to get out there and probably could become professional. We knew we had something special and, instead of building with people who came on board to help us, we self-destructed and self-sabotaged. We were offered help every step of the way, but we didn't trust to go with our hearts, flow with these excited souls, and take every opportunity given to us. We destroyed ourselves from within because the two most creative thinkers of the band could not find a way through. What it needed was for me and the other peaceful members of the band to be able to draw these guys to come together and help each other work through the problem, but I was not level-headed enough and nor was anyone else. We also needed to make business decisions in a strategic, mature and unrushed manner. The original bass player (still also a good friend) who could have helped, had left, to go and grow vegetables and live off the land, but had probably predicted the disaster ahead! We needed techniques to learn how to work together as a team; we needed to build a strong unit as one, bring in systems of how to create a community, to help

> *...telling musicians in a band not to take drugs is like telling a cat not to chase mice.*

face the same way. We were all highly charged, emotional and quite messed-up people, on personal paths of self-discovery. If only we had had a model, a way to work with each other, that would have helped us climb to higher levels and keep pushing the momentum.

If you're going to take drugs, it needs to be done carefully around the band. We will cover this in a later chapter, but this is my example of why drugs are really, really not good for building a band. Of course, in moderation, they are OK, but every week, or several times a week, like we were doing, is definitely not good nor is it going to advance your career!

However, telling musicians in a band not to take drugs is like telling a cat not to chase mice. The fact is that many bands do take drugs. So, the paramount advice is, if you are going to take them, be honest with yourselves and your bandmates. If you are on a comedown from the weekend DO NOT make fundamental decisions, wait for a period of sobriety or when people are actually NOT on a comedown!

If you have big business decisions to make; strategy, PR stuff to do, anything that you don't naturally do well, then do not take drugs for a short period (preferably using foresight and maintaining clean times for some weeks in busy organisational periods) as they will disrupt your flow.

If only we had had access/known about Zone Technique, the way to conduct band rehearsals, or any of the tools or advice in this book, that band *may* have been so different.

Part of my motivation for writing these words is because I see bands making the same mistakes over and over again. These are obvious things that happen when faced with the kind of stressful life that you have as a musician. So, please be centred, take days to think about big decisions. But there's more of this later in the section about MAKING DECISIONS!

The second example is from after I moved off the drum throne and stepped into band management. One of the first bands I managed was a lo-fi, blues rock band.

Well, when I got on board, there were positive signs that they could do very well. I knew them from the live dance act days in Leeds. We also beat them in the same battle of the bands where we beat Parva (Kaiser Chiefs)! After several years, we had managed to set up licensing deals around the world; they were touring in many territories, but they still had day jobs as much of the money coming in was going out again to invest in new videos, recordings, art and touring costs. We were making all content in the UK, on their independent label, and then licensing to all the global licensee labels. Of course getting paid, especially by the major labels, was a year or two away!

The band had its own record label, and the only full-time member of the band was me, as the manager. I was working around the clock for the band and there was another fine gent, who also had a job, but ran the record label. He was a great guy and put a lot of work into the project. The guitarist, songwriter, owner of the label and creative controller of the project wanted to be in control of everything. He had trust issues insofar as, he thought no one would understand him or his vision, or people would not do their jobs properly and that unless he controlled everything and kept a close eye on it all, and micromanaged everything, then it would all collapse. I believe that the self-fulfilling prophecy is strong and often we create our own reality. So, as executive of the record label, songwriter, musical director, artwork designer, in charge of CD manufacturing, exec producer of recording, mixing, making videos, touring and being overall dictator, whilst having a full-time job, he eventually had a nervous breakdown.

This is a lesson in trusting that you have to bring people in and work collaboratively with others, and the way that we do that is paramount to the health of the project. None of them had any mindfulness practice; again there were a lot of knee-jerk reactions going on in this band.

One such example, and my biggest error for this same band, was being coaxed into sacking the bass player who was taking a lot of magic mushrooms and was very unreliable. He would miss soundchecks for gigs, because he was sleeping off a high, and he would regularly have to be retrieved from his bed to get to any band appointment. This was not acceptable at the level the band were at, and I would say, at any level, if a band wants to progress. Unfortunately, just before their biggest tour, where we were off to Japan to play the massive Summer Sonic Festival and sign a deal with EMI Japan, we fired him. I regret that decision to this day, as he was a massive part of the band's brand. With hindsight, we needed to find a way that would work to communicate where the band was at and how we needed him to behave.

I was being asked to do it by the guitarist/singer-songwriter, main guy/dictator and I was weak, lacking confidence and was passive-aggressive at that point. It was my first foray into management, the first band I'd managed on a full-time basis, and I was foolish to listen. However, had the main man not been such a control freak and made the bass player more of a band member with responsibilities other than simply playing (he was an extremely witty poet who self-published his own book of poetry), then perhaps the whole scenario/dynamic would have played out differently too.

There is always a third way. We tend to react to things with anger or frustration and from that place we will never choose the right path. We feel like someone has wronged us, so we feel vengeful, OR we blame ourselves and so we want to give too much or do ourselves down.

The third way is unemotional, thoughtful and insightful. Using the motive 'how can we make this work for the higher purpose?', I advise taking away ALL aspects of ego and the feeling of being wronged. The way to do this, is to 'get out of your own way'. Instead of thinking about that victimhood, think about what you could have done differently and also focus on the other person/people involved. Instead of blaming them, try and understand what has led up to this situation. Try and understand why they may be feeling the way they are and what you can do to change the circumstances. To be able to look at a situation from many sides is a necessary skill to develop, therefore become focused on finding a solution that is centred only on the best outcome for the greater good.

To elevate the argument to a higher purpose, it is too easy to get stuck in the idea that I do everything and they do nothing – we only know what gifts that person brings when they are no longer there. Particularly in the strange dynamics of bands, we should only really focus on 'how is this band of people going to achieve its goal?'. I realised that the bass player, in the last example, brought an amazing showmanship, enthusiasm, style and 'branding' (he was well over 6 foot, had blonde dreadlocks, covered his double bass perfectly in leopard skin and always wore long shorts on stage), his musicianship, silliness and presence were amazing and was totally unrivalled by any of his replacements. Ultimately, by firing him, I believe, we contributed to the beginning of the end of the band.

It's best if we realise early on that there are such subtle energies at work in the dynamics of a band and its organisation that you have to be extremely careful when you're talking about firing someone. I have NEVER seen a sacking work (meaning helping a band rise to the next level) in a band that has turned semi-professional or professional! I think this is, in part, due to the attitude that leads up to a sacking and the aftermath. The nature of firing someone means that people have been looking with eyes of blame, that it's not good enough. Once one person is sacked and may have been a scapegoat for other underlying issues in the band, then who's to say it will stop there? I think that a sacking can be a poisoned chalice that ultimately destroys the fabric of the band; the rich tapestry and dynamic that makes the band.

> *...there are such subtle energies at work in the dynamics of a band and its organisation...*

Therefore, working through your problems with the person involved... using the techniques advised, so far and later in this book, is always going to be healthier and will make you stronger. In my opinion, you are more likely to succeed that way than if you sack someone. Make the problems they create a band problem rather than their problem.

This is the string that comes from the live dance music project and runs through into this last example too.

It is very difficult to decipher the incredible dynamic that makes up a successful band, and we could theorise about that for a few more chapters! All I know, for sure, is that one element of that is definitely respect, even if it wavers, it is there deep down; there is always a mutual respect in bands and band members that go the distance. I would suggest that successful bands would, consciously or subconsciously, try to find a third way to address problems.

The obvious way to address problems is to get rid of them, bury them, pretend they do not exist. It is easy to blame the band's problems on someone who is constantly late, or the person who is always finding issues. We all need to look at ourselves first and ask:

- What do I do that encourages that person's difficult behaviour?
- What else do they bring to the table in terms of the art?

Also, if you think they don't bring much, maybe that is the point! Maybe everyone else brings a lot and you need a more passive member for the dynamic!

Always beware that the knee-jerk reaction is not the way forward.

There should be a session, once a month, where the band sits down and does the following exercise:

EXERCISE: Sit in a circle and pair up. If there is an odd number of you then one group of three is fine. You will all swap until everyone has done the exercise with everyone else. This is something you can do away from the rehearsal room, when you are in the pub, at a festival or in a meeting and not under time pressure.

Sit opposite your partner and say the following statements:

1. **"I love you brother/sister because/when…"** this should be done three times, i.e. three reasons why you love them
2. **"I dislike you brother/sister when you/because…"** this should be done three times, i.e. three reasons why you dislike them
3. **"I would like you to be more…"** x three if possible
4. **"I would like you to be less…"** x three if possible

The best bands will have such honest relationships that they can say anything to each other. As soon as someone in the group is scared of saying something to someone else, then you will have bitching, festering problems and poisonous situations. I strongly encourage you to say the unsayable in this situation. Break down barriers and borders, leave nothing to fester. Whoever is on the receiving end of this (you all will be) must be strong, accept the feedback/criticism with love and feel appreciative for the fact that someone is calling them out on their shit!

If this is all new and scary, well, get used to it. It is best to be told this stuff by people close to you. Perhaps NO ONE has EVER said any of these things to you before! Well, what a good time to start! We can learn that none of us are so important that we can't be told by someone else when we are being a dick OR how great we are at something. The sooner you lose your ego amongst band members, the better the band can run. Once we know that Chris is always a dick when it comes to money, we can laugh about it. If Chris can laugh about it too, then Chris can either improve with his new-found awareness, or we are all aware of it and we can make provisions for it, so that he doesn't get the opportunity to spend the whole band's petrol money on weed and booze!

As a band, if you want longevity you are going to face days with little sleep, intense travel and some very testing relationships with the outside world; namely business people. You need to be prepared for this. If you become a strong unit, where you have confronted each other's darkness and light, and outed each other's most difficult characteristics, you lay solid foundations for being a group/force to be reckoned with. You can become a unit that is unwavering in its strength for each other.

Please always consider the third way: the way that you can't think of immediately. If it is suggested that either we do this or that – A or B – they are the obvious choices. Be cautious of settling with these options. When you are dealing with a band, you're dealing with a very delicate ecosystem.

The only way that you're going to achieve longevity is by being a team of people who are able to own your feelings, as individuals, and solve problems TOGETHER. The sooner you use your creative brains, looking for solutions rather than starting to look at each other as a problem, the quicker and easier you

> *As a band, if you want longevity you are going to face days with little sleep, intense travel and some very testing relationships*

will rise up the ladder.

If you can find creative ways of dealing with your problems, which are not knee-jerk reactions and which do not end up affecting the band, you will succeed because that is the clever way. It's not A or B… but C.

The point of the third way is for all band members to own their own feelings, their own anger. No one *makes* you angry. You feel anger because you react to something that you don't like. If you do not express your feelings that anger will not escape from your body and mind and it will become more powerful. More frustration and anger will persist and the more you do not express it, the more the monster grows.

When I was in the first year of university, I did what many students do. I was thrown credit cards in freshers' week. Across the course of that year, I racked up about £1,800 on the credit cards, and of course, at the time, I had A LOT of fun. However, I ignored the monthly payments I was meant to be paying each month, probably not being able to afford them without more debt. By the end of the year, the debt had grown and grown towards the £3,000 mark. I was fortunate enough to be bailed out by my parents, but on the proviso that I cut up the credit cards and never used credit cards again! To this day, I still do not use credit cards and have no debt, because I see debt as a monster that grows and grows!

So back to our example of how anger may grow into a monster in your music career…

Jim is your assigned merch stall person. But Jim is short of cash and is offered some weed by one of his mates. You have been on the road a while, he gets overexcited and he buys more than he should. He uses merch money, with every intention of giving it back, although it is debatable whether that is realistic any time soon! He has lifted £90 from the band. Of course, everyone finds out pretty soon and people get angry. Maybe that was money that was going to be used for food, or savings, and someone says, "Why the hell didn't you just ask, first?" (Probably because some people would have told him to f*** off!)

So, there is anger and frustration here, after all, this is not the first time Jim has done this. It is pretty typical Jim behaviour and, quite frankly, people are growing sick and tired of it. BUT it is a rare occasion when anyone actually tells him. Of course, everyone is scared of confrontation and no one wants to rock the boat. The anger has built up and if anyone does say anything now, it is likely to blow up and the results could be frightening. So, instead of speaking out the anger/frustration is building up. Because people are beginning to get frightened and scared of this growing monster, they start talking amongst themselves and all of a sudden, before we know it, there is quite a lot of bitching going on!

As you can imagine, this is not a healthy scenario. Perhaps you have even experienced this?

So, let's look at an alternative way of dealing with an issue, before the monster grows...

This situation, and any other that brings anger, can be dealt with in the following way. You have to call this person and sit down with them, either individually or as a group. If you do it as a group, then you must use the protocol of one person speaking at a time. You can work out who is going to start, but anyone that feels anger must have their say within the same structure as below...

The structure comes from an NVC technique by

Marshall B Rosenberg which appears in his 1998 book, *Non-Violent Communication: A Language of Life* (PuddleDancer Press, Encinitas, CA, USA). I highly recommend it, as there are many other techniques in there too, but I apply his ideas in the example below:

- Tell Jim *what* happened (data)
- Tell Jim how *you* feel. "*I feel*" statement – by doing this you are *owning* the feeling *you* have
- Tell *him* why it makes *you* feel like this

then

- What *you need* e.g. "*I would like/my request is…*"

So, the chat looks like this:

"Jim, come sit down, we need to speak to you. I am going to start, but I believe some other people have stuff to say. We'll speak one by one, please acknowledge you have heard, and we'll have space for you to speak your mind when you have heard and acknowledged everyone. Is that OK?"

Assume Jim agrees, maybe he sighs a bit or looks quite embarrassed because he knows he is in for something!

- "Jim, you stole £90 from the merch money to buy weed"
- "I am upset that you didn't come to ask the other band members for the cash, we could have all chipped in!
- "I feel like I can't trust you properly any more, and I feel disrespected because that merch money belongs

to all of us and we also have debts to pay off from it.

- "I would like you to put the money straight back from the very next money you receive in payment and PROMISE that if you ever need/want money from any band funds that you come and check with band members first. PLEEEEEEEASE."

You may also make a reasonable request from Jim, something that he can do for the rest of the band that shows some sacrifice and giving on his behalf, as a way of showing his apology in action.

Jim should agree to these terms. And it should BE A WARNING to any 'JIMS' in the band that, *"you must not break this promise, the more you break these promises, the more your trust credits with the band run thin."*

Trust:

Trust is probably the most powerful bonding tool you have. Consequently, because it is such a strong bonding tool, it can also be a destroyer.

I recently read a beautiful piece called 'Love & Trust' from the Chabad.org website by Tzvi Freeman.[2]

"Trust is the child of love, for where love showers down, trust will grow. And since it is a child, the reciprocal is also true: As the child's call awakens a parent from deep sleep, so trust awakens the love that gave birth to it. Provide love; trust will be born..."

So, let's expand a bit on this idea. Love is the unconditional giving to others. This fosters deep trust. The more you open up to others and show you trust and love them, the stronger the bond is. You can, of course, reverse this process, simply by doing the opposite!

So, let's go to a real example from my life, where I managed to disobey all of the wisdoms espoused in this book. I made the mistakes so you don't have to!

The third example in this chapter, from my band life, is back to a band with whom I was drumming; it was a live hip-hop band also based in Leeds. We were a six-piece band with horns, that mixed jazz, funk and hard hip-hop beats. The vibe was very special; audiences would generally go pretty nuts. From a technical and electric point of view, it was probably the best band I was in. Most of the musicians have gone on to be pro and one is now a three-time Grammy Award winner!

I guess it was my first kind of experience of management as well. Very low-level management in booking rehearsals, getting some gigs and generally making things happen away from the music creation. Except for the bass player, who was over all the time, we all lived together. It was all very good and we had great times, an incredible house – a mansion in the countryside, with electric gates, two lounges (one of which we made into a studio), huge kitchen, two gardens… We played music ALL the time and when we weren't playing, we were listening to music, smoking, drinking and 'being a band'. It was an incredible experience.

We had the opportunity of releasing a single on the label of a friend, who was actually in the lo-fi blues rock band, and every time we talked about releasing the single there was a little bit of anxiety there from the rapper. She also worked in a shop for a fraction of the hourly rate that the rest of us were getting from peripatetic teaching and playing gigs.

She was more than capable of teaching, as she had been to music college, studying guitar and vocal, but she didn't want to. She would come in from 8 hours in the shop knackered. We would have been playing music, we would have three grooves written and we'd invite her to come and jam in the evening, and she would refuse and go and watch 'Buffy' with her girlfriend.

Of course, we had set band rehearsal times that she would adhere to and then we would work very well together. The only time this made any sense to me was at the end of our explosive row about the single release. She said, "Brett, don't you get it? I just don't believe in making money out of music!" That was that, my heart jumped out of my body, landed on the floor and felt like it had been trampled on 1,000 times!

Nowadays, I realise that although her approach was different, we could have probably navigated it, somehow, creatively. She was playing the long, long game. Realistically, it would have been some years that we would have had to struggle before we could 'make it'. Had the band and I been more mature and willing to chat and discuss and find the third way, no doubt we could have resolved it. But my reaction was to shout back, be in pain and, ultimately, quit the band and go into management!

I was 26, the other guys were 23. I felt at 26 that time was running out and I needed other skills. Thankfully, a friend of mine, whose sister I was going to manage, took me out to lunch. He was an amazing bass player but had also recently finished a law conversion. He questioned me. "So I hear you are going to manage my sister." (With whom I had spent many years at university, encouraging her to sing professionally because she used to blow everyone's minds.) I said "yes" and he said "but you don't really know what you are doing do you?", I said "no!" and he said, "well let me help you then!". He was willing to spend hours and days a week with me, training me in music law, management and the music industry in general. Without him, it would have been a much harder path and, maybe, might not happened at all for me. He had a flat in Great Titchfield Street, London, W1, where I would hang out with him and learn about the music business. It would become our office address and Monumental Management was born. I would manage 13 acts and things would continue that way for the next 13 years! But, I do always wonder what would have happened IF we had found another way to navigate our issues in the hip-hop band. It was one of those bands that just worked. People were excited by it and, to this day, I still listen to a live gig we did and think, what if I had had all this knowledge then that I am writing about now!

So just remember guys, if you knee-jerk, if you go: A or B and you don't look seriously, considering other options, if you fly off the handle and shout and scream, it is never going to come good. You need to make delicate and clever decisions. You need to use the Zone Technique, you need to think, you need to breathe, you need to stop, be mindful of your decisions and work as a team.

This goes for your relationship with business people as well. There is never any need to shout at anyone; there is no need to lose it with people, there is no need to be rude. The way to go is to think and make sure that you are making decisions from your highest self, which means that you need time, to be calm and not to be stressing. You need to use the

Zone Technique and unblock your stress points in your body. You need to be coming from a calm place with no anxiety: not A or B but the C way. The C way is the third way; the C way is the clever and calm way.

I heard a story that my friend told me recently that illustrates this. There was a successful media mogul, who climbed the ladder and made millions. My friend worked with him and always found him rude and arrogant. He saw him many years later, after they had finished working together. The media mogul seemed approachable and kind. My friend said he walked away from the conversation with a smile when the mogul said, amongst other things, "You know, if I could do it all again, I would have preferred to not be rude. If there is one thing that I have learned – there is no need to shout or be rude or abusive to people." I agree!

CHAPTER 6

'Drugs Are Bad Mkay?'

It is time to tackle the all-important thing that plagues our lives as musicians – drugs.

I think one of the reasons why we all used to do, or still do, far too many drugs as musicians is because we are either insecure, creative beings or have soft boundaries, creatively looking to push the envelope in every way!

Another reason why we may use drugs is because we overthink and we are in our heads a lot, and what drugs tend to do is shut off the conscious mind and allow our subconscious to flow, giving us a break from our heads. Ah, that flow state is so nice isn't it? Well, that is the place we are getting to with our Zone Technique now. Yes, it is not as easy, or as quick! But, you can get there…

What the Zone Technique will give you is harder to attain because you're not putting something in your nose or smoking something. You have to decide to focus on yourself, go and sit somewhere, and reset and concentrate on only observing.

ZONE TECHNIQUE REMINDER:

- **Sit comfortably, close your eyes**
- **Concentrate on one thing only – observe breath or visualising/observing an area of the body**
- **Do not try and change it, just observe it without doing anything**
- **Check that your breathing is regular and deep**
- **Continue this for 10-20 mins**

Put another way, and more analytically, in order to create, we need to live in chaos, make sense of the chaos and create order out of it. That is what beautiful art is, order from chaos. As I said in the introduction: *"As an artist today you need to do what artists do best, which is embody the chaos and out of that chaos create order. You need to battle with your greatest fears of constantly stepping into the unknown, to express yourself on the rest of society's behalf that which is not spoken. But, you also need to have your hand on your business. After being in the chaotic space, you need to be at the meeting at 10 a.m., on time, with a smile on your face, or the people who will help run your business won't work with you!"*

One of the things that leads us to being a musician is the idea that, somehow, we don't quite fit in and we have different ideas from the rest of the population. I never really dreamed of becoming a professional in any other field than music.

I think we have to realise that we are a different species and that one of the reasons why we do the drugs is for escape. We seek happiness in creation and it delivers, but when we are not creating – and inevitably receiving love from people for being recognised as creative beings – we seek that pleasure elsewhere.

And so here begins a lesson about drugs!

In this chapter, I will be frank about my own drug use and talk about personal experiences and personal opinions. I think that since I was taking drugs regularly in the 1990s and 2000s, all drugs have become much stronger and the drugs market has changed significantly. I would advise that if you are going to take drugs, you carefully read the advice available from places like Talk to Frank and The Loop. They are there to help support people who are taking drugs, and you can find out about what drugs do, and how much is safe to take.

I think whatever your policy towards drugs, it is extremely important to have extended periods of sobriety. Obviously sobriety and then binging is not acceptable as it is life threatening and unfortunately some of our best musicians have shortened their lives by doing this, so please don't do that! Moderate use of these toxins followed by sustained periods of sobriety is probably best **IF** you think you wish to use any of them.

Essentially, what I am saying is, just don't take much of these most of the time. If you find yourself doing any of the below daily or even weekly, then you are probably trying to mask some character flaw or hide something about yourself that you don't like or can't cope with, perhaps, even from yourself!

Now, even though I do on occasions do many of the below, I am going to tell you all the reasons why you *shouldn't* do any of the drugs below! The reason? Because, it is good for us to take a moment to face some truths, for all of us, to understand the consequences and to have an opportunity to explore honestly, truthfully, inside ourselves. We should all be asking ourselves questions. I am completely non-judgemental, I am offering you a chance to put yourself on trial in a private space while reading this and afterwards, just to consider what your truth really is and how you should be approaching any of the vices below.

The last thing to say here, before we get into the 'nitty-gritty', is that I have purposely left out prescription drugs from this chapter. I would hope that if you are on prescription drugs you are under the supervision of a medical professional and registered as so, and consulting with your doctor **IF** you are ill-advisedly taking *any* of the drugs I talk about.

Cannabis/Weed:

Yes 'the green', 'the herb', 'ganja'. Everyone is smoking it, so surely it makes us more creative? In small amounts, it can help switch the emphasis of the mind and make certain potentially useful brain functions accessible. BUT, you need to know, and be pretty specific about it, in the first instance; the actual type of weed you are smoking. If you smoke it all the time, then like any drug, your tolerance level builds and before you know it, you need it just to feel 'normal'/functional. So, if you give up smoking weed for a month and do some exercise, you will see a difference in your abilities, your creative drive and your drive for life. Therefore, I say "No way does it make us more creative in the long term".

Perhaps, if you are already an incredibly creative being and you

> " *I will be frank about my own drug use and talk about personal experiences and personal opinions...*

smoke pure weed on occasion, it will make you a little more creative than you were and it will unlock some creativity, shake off some insecurities and make you feel liberated. But that is the reason why we are doing the Zone Technique, it is doing the same thing, but the Zone Technique is more sustainable! The Zone Technique is unlocking something that is already inside you and, I would strongly argue, pumping the cannabinoids and THC into your system is not doing you as much good as Zone Technique and mindfulness practice. Instead, smoking weed (especially with tobacco in it) is making you reliant on the weed to access a place that is there for the taking for FREE.

In fact, what this is doing to you is taking you away from your true soul essence. It is escapism, it is dulling the senses, it is making you less productive, it is costing you money and it's a distraction.

Before we continue, and you start citing the Rasta community and Bob Marley, let's cover this NOW before you switch off and think I am talking rubbish!

Firstly, Bob Marley and the Rasta community of Jamaica usually smoke PURE WEED, or hashish, that is grown organically outdoors!

If you are only smoking pure weed (not skunk or any kind of hybrid) then I will adjust the above and say that, in moderation, it can help you attain a different perspective and help you create, but I know that the vast percentage of people reading this book will be smoking tobacco with the weed. This is a completely different drug that delivers the THC in the weed to the body and mind – at faster rates – and, therefore, dulls the senses and makes us less sensitive and less in touch with ourselves.

As I said above, if one smokes all the time, then you need to smoke to access creativity. It is also about association – if, over years, one gets used to smoking before creating, then this is a habit-forming exercise and, of course, you will need weed to create. I am suggesting that a period of sobriety, using the Zone Technique will help to remove this addiction from your life and will save you a load of money in the process!

Why do we really like it after a gig, for example? Because we're really high and this will dull us a bit, so it makes us a little less high so we don't feel as weird?

A friend of mine had the same dealer who used to deal to a famous, world-renowned, scratch DJ. The dealer told my friend a story about him… This DJ explained the reason why he was no longer buying weed from the dealer. He explained that he thought he was really good, but the one thing he knew that made him great was when he STOPPED smoking weed.

This is an important quote from Marianne Williamson, the American spiritual teacher, author and lecturer, that I think is extremely poignant and can be relevant when you find yourself needing to dull your senses after being high from a gig:

"Our deepest fear is not that we are inadequate. Our deepest fear is that we are powerful beyond measure. It is our light, not our darkness that most frightens us."

Implying that when we are truly shining, we don't quite know what to do with ourselves. Have you ever heard people say "I have to smoke, it calms me down"!

She goes on to say…

"We ask ourselves, Who am I to be brilliant, gorgeous, talented, and fabulous? Actually, who are you not to be? You are a child of God."

Yes! Don't fear your true light and gifts…

"Your playing small does not serve the world. There is nothing enlightened about shrinking so that other people will not feel insecure around you. We are all meant to shine, as children do. We were born to make manifest the glory of God that is within us."

You feel you need to hide your gifts, or are embarrassed at being too bright, or somehow have a self-destructive or self-sabotaging streak. In some way, we are scared of our own success.

"It is not just in some of us; it is in everyone and as we let our own light shine, we unconsciously give others permission to do the same. As we are liberated from our own fear, our presence automatically liberates others."[3] Marianne Williamson – *A Return To Love: Reflections on the Principles of A Course in Miracles*, Harper Collins, 1992. From Chapter 7, Section 3 (Pg. 190-191).

There are sections of society that believe weed helps creativity. I am not going to try and debunk this. However, I will suggest that those that use it as a creative drug smoke it completely pure. NO tobacco with it. If you smoke pure weed and find it works for you, then ok. There is a theme with this section that you'll see. I just ask you to be honest with yourself and ask the question *Why am I doing this? Is it for escape, or is it because I really like it and it helps me create? What would happen if I didn't do it for a while? Have I ever tried sobriety?!*

Just be honest with yourself. Make sure you are not taking drugs to escape your awful reality. That is the strongest advice I can give here.

Now, If you are producing high art on weed, then why not make it a bit more scientific and experiment? After all, it's just a month of your life. How about this: try not to smoke at all (no weed, no tobacco, no drugs) for 4 weeks, do daily exercise (at least 20 minutes of raising your heart rate) and use the Zone Technique daily for at least 20 minutes, especially before creating – and see if you produce even higher art!

So many musicians talk about their mental health issues and a number one question from me is, "Do you smoke weed?" More often than not, the answer is YES! So I just say, "WELL STOP SMOKING WEED!"

If you are a happy person and all is well, OK. But a daily habit – several joints every day habitually and loads at the weekend and oh look, you have mental health issues!

You see what tends to happen with regular weed smokers is you don't focus as well and apply yourself as well. Then you don't get as much done or have the energy and motivation to do everything you would like to achieve, so this leads to self-loathing! It's a downwards spiral. IF YOU ARE UNHAPPY WITH YOURSELF AND OTHERS AND YOU SMOKE WEED, then just STOP!

Do whatever it takes to stop. Avoid people who smoke, don't buy it! Just stop for a month and see the difference in your life and get some daily, rigorous exercise, which will help everything! Within approximately 21 days you will see a BIG difference!

Before you tell me you are one of those weed smokers that is really productive when you smoke, I will ask you some key questions to answer honestly to yourself:

- Do I smoke so much that I actually need the weed to get me into a place of productivity?
- When was the last time I had a sustained period of not smoking weed?
- How much better would I be, if for a number of months I didn't smoke?
- Do I owe it to myself to kick weed out for a time to really explore what my true capabilities are?

You should also use these questions in respect of any other drug you use regularly including tobacco and alcohol.

Cocaine:

Have you ever watched *Narcos* the series that was on Netflix? If you have you will see that cocaine only became so predominantly used in the West because our friends – the drug cartels in South America – decided that they could make a lot of money out of people. The brilliant actor and stand-up comedian Robin Williams once joked in one of his stand-up routines (in the 80s when he was struggling with addiction himself), he said, speaking in a South American accent: "COCAINE?! Ah, cocaine is our gift to the white man for what he did to uuuus!"

The whole win for the cocaine dealer is that the hit is relatively short, it releases just enough dopamine, energy and 'buzz' to make it extremely addictive, so that the user wants more and the person selling the cocaine can make lots of money from you!

I am not going to pretend that I don't do it, I do, occasionally, it is normally for functional reasons. I have a theory – if you need to bring the fun, all it will do is make you feel a bit nicer and give you energy, but it is not going to bring any fun, that and the good chat, is up to you. It seems a shame it costs so much for just a bit of energy and a dopamine hit. I can feel the same after a really great workout! Basically, it keeps you awake and functioning. I use it to drain the last drops out of a party, because we have been drinking for several hours and there is a bunch of good friends who I will not see again this year, that kind of scenario.

It steals creativity and awareness while you are on it and gives very little, especially after sustained use. Its addictiveness is DANGEROUS too. How can something not that great, be soooo addictive! Even writing this, I think, *well, one line would be quite nice now, wouldn't it?* NO! Because it never is just one line! Just learn that lesson for free, instead of spending literally thousands of pounds on it. Buy some new equipment and every time you use it, you can thank your lucky stars and pat yourself on the back that you didn't snort it up your nose. It's really nowhere near the sustained buzz you can get from using the Zone Technique and THEN playing music.

For a creative being, there is no way you are going to produce great creative work on this drug. BUT not just that, it is also going to stay in your system for some time to come and is going to wreck your creative juices for at least the next few days and, if you have had a session, it can be a week before you start being able to reach your potential again.

I am going to labour the point here and stick on the bad white powder topic; it is keeping in mind the power of the evil white stuff that I must spend another couple of paragraphs on the subject!

Luckily, many of us don't earn very much money so we can't afford the habit (at least being broke is good for something!). However, I've seen people on that slippery slope and, pretty soon, instead of just being a weekend thing it becomes an every week thing. It can then easily become a midweek thing, because you start now on Thursdays, then you suddenly start on Wednesdays and, before you know it, you are spending £150 a week on this stuff and you're an addict. If you are touring, you've got money in your pocket and you're bored with the gig, it is very easy to get caught in this way.

I would suggest that if you recognise yourself slipping down this path, you need to get into EXERCISE as soon as possible and you need to have as much of an addiction for exercise as you have for cocaine, which means that four times a week you are doing some form of intensive exercise, at least raising your heart rate for 20 minutes+ per day to start with, rising up to an hour per day. This will give you a buzz and help you to combat your addiction.

> *...addiction is so common is because we are all frail humans. We all make mistakes...*

The only long-lasting effects that cocaine will have on your life will be that it will make you think that you are amazingly creative and that you are incredible at what you do. It will also drain your bank balance and give you regrets that you invested so much time and money in an empty vice that left you with nothing. You will probably find your decision-making acutely affected. Cocaine (and most drugs) play havoc with your prefrontal cortex (the part of the brain where decisions are made). Making bad decisions, thinking about coke a lot, spending your hard-earned money on it, getting addicted (even if you don't want to admit it) and having your decision-making affected, as well as not sleeping properly, are just some of the issues.

Can you see, by adding these factors together, how easy it will be to find your entire life in complete chaos? Hanging on to life with your fingernails! PLEASE, if you find yourself in this situation right now, don't be scared to ask your friends, bandmates and anyone else you know for help. You have only made a mistake that some of the greatest artists of all time have made.

The reason why addiction is so common is because we are all frail humans. We all make mistakes. We often suffer from self-hate, insecurity and low confidence. YOU ARE NOT ALONE. I have certainly had, and do have, times when I feel like that. "Oh, I screwed up again! OK great, how did I get here again?" After screwing up so much, making amends and then screwing up again in a different way, we soon learn and, therefore, just get better at accepting that that is part of life.

This is a phrase that will be repeated in this book, but it seems appropriate to say it now, as a mantra that I gift to you when times are a challenge.

THE STRUGGLE IS THE CHALLENGE AND THE CHALLENGE IS A GIFT FOR US TO GROW.

It depends why you think you're on this earth but, as I said earlier, it is a core belief of mine that we are here to learn, grow, get better, become higher, more at peace, refine ourselves and GIVE our gifts to others. For me, that makes the point of living much more meaningful and, after all, without meaning, we will die. (I say this with real conviction), the psychotherapist Viktor Frankl, who I quoted earlier in this book, wrote a whole book on the subject, which I highly recommend! *Man's Search for Meaning* – Viktor E Frankl (1946) Verlag für Jugend und Volk (Austria).

So, the creations that you thought were 'amazing' when you were high on coke, will only be that amazing while you are on the cocaine. As soon as you finish, you start self-deprecating and thinking that actually it, and you, are not that amazing at all, which is a shame, because the fact that you are feeling low and being self-deprecating means you actually do care about self-improvement, that you are interested in how to make yourself a better person and you are a creator of art – your gift which you are offering to the people – which means that you are COMPLETELY AMAZING!

You know, every time I have done cocaine, I always think everything should go really well, because it feels so good when that initial buzz kicks off. On reflection, I realise that nothing has gone as well as it could have gone had I not been on it. I mean interactions with people, my awareness, my sharpness, real focus and natural ability, are actually, counter-intuitively, dulled. The one use for cocaine is to help you stay awake! Really, beyond that, it doesn't add value. It gives you energy and you think that with the energy and a dopamine injection everything is great. BUT actually, you take away the power of your higher energies, and people can feel the 'coke vibe' a mile off, especially if you have fallen into the trap of doing lots of it. If you need to stay awake there are plenty of legal pharmaceuticals for that.

Ecstasy:

I must say at this point; I do not condone the use of Ecstasy or any drug for that matter. The views expressed here are entirely personal based on my own feelings and experiences. I cannot speak for the reader or anyone else except for myself!

Wow! What a drug! I love Ecstasy! I would love to be able to do Ecstasy without the comedown the next week!

When I went to university I couldn't talk to girls very easily, I couldn't hug girls. I couldn't interact with people comfortably at all and I was very insecure. I did my first Ecstasy pill in the late '90s at university – in fact, at the end of the first week of my first year! I was invited to a techno rave and I was hugging girls, then I was dancing, hugging, laughing, chatting and smiling, and I genuinely felt incredible, absolutely incredible!

I loved it – I have to say I absolutely loved it – and I realised pretty quickly that what I was being shown through this experience, existed inside me. It was an inspiration, I felt like I was witnessing the possibilities in life and the possibilities in me. It gave me immense confidence and I loved it.

It was like I could see everything that I needed to know, about the world, the universe, life and myself, all at once.

I tried to cling on to those thoughts when I was back in the reality of every day, learn from the experience, and that's the thing that I have tried to learn from all drugs. The only issue with Ecstasy is that, after taking it for a while, the comedown the following week is hard. I talked about this a bit earlier, and how it affected the various band experiences I had. It can be extremely damaging to dynamics if several band members are taking Ecstasy regularly, as you will be experiencing group comedowns and, as mentioned, it is important to recognise that you are in a low place. No big decisions should be made, and everyone needs to check themselves before getting angry at a fellow band member!

The best description of the effects of Ecstasy is from my good friend, who painted the following picture… "It's like everything you need to know about the nature of the universe and your own soul, and the world is there for you to see so clearly, except there is a wall in front of you. Ecstasy is like you have wheeled a trampoline in front of the wall and you are jumping up and down so that you can see over the wall, and you witness all of the secrets that you need to know about everything, almost complete enlightenment. It's all so clear! But one day, you must take away the trampoline and climb the wall!"

So, when you stop being high, the wall is still there and you can no longer see over it, although you may have memories and those small memories can have a positive effect on your daily life if there were things you saw that really resonated within you. But, if you really want to reach those same highs in your daily life, without needing drugs and having to battle through a comedown etc., then one day you have to move the trampoline to the side and climb the wall! (Which, of course, is hard because it can be a big, tall wall!)

Therefore, I think Ecstasy is amazing and, on occasion, a great experience (perhaps I do it once or twice a year now) but it's unsustainable. If you are going to get the real gifts from Ecstasy, then try and learn from it. Analyse things while you are on it and, afterwards, try and learn to become a better human through its use, remembering that you only feel so shitty the next week because you have less serotonin in your brain. Well that's OK, and it's going to come back when you eat some bananas. Do some exercise and don't do it again for a while!

Acid/Mushrooms:

For me, this is by far and away the most spiritual drug to enjoy and from which to learn. The first lesson from these drugs to accept is that if you have any hesitation or doubt that you cannot dispel easily or quickly, then I wouldn't bother. Imagine you are signing up to go on a mental roller coaster for several hours (sometimes as many as 10 hours!), you need to be very up for the journey. There should be no hesitation, you must think *YES! I really want to be on a trip right now.* The best description I have heard of acid was by Timothy Leary. He says that acid/most psychedelics destroy the 'reality map' (everything we have built up in our lives and believed to be true/real) and replace it with question marks and the ability to look at absolutely everything with a different perspective. I would make sure you have controlled your environment: make sure that you are with people with whom you are 100% comfortable – a small group – that you have a private location that you really like, in a place where you feel protected, and then

> **Ecstasy is like you have wheeled a trampoline in front of the wall and you are jumping up and down so that you can see over it...**

you can enjoy yourself – and enjoy it you will – but again, not all the time, but in healthy moderation, then enjoy the exploration! Sorry, but my disclaimer is that if you are of a fragile mental health and you are not particularly happy then you MUST NOT do this drug, absolutely not. You can only do this drug when you are feeling good, you feel of a reasonably happy disposition and secure in your life. It's OK if you are prepared to just go with it and have a laugh, but you can also see life from very different perspectives.

Ketamine:

My advice is the same as above, except that you should do very, very, small amounts of this. Do not do huge lines, as lots of people do, because it will send you into a 'K-hole' and you won't be able to do anything. Very, very, very, small amounts and control your environment, as it is a hugely psychedelic experience. It can also give you bad bladder problems! NO ALCOHOL with this drug. It has become popular to take lots of this stuff and be in a club. I think this is a bad idea, as it is tantamount to being whacked over the head and left stumbling around a strange environment. This is not the cleverest of plans and can lead you into trouble. I would make sure your environment is controlled, you are around people you trust and you don't do massive amounts, the true benefits come from small amounts throughout an evening.

So, actually psychedelics can be interesting to explore and may well give you a different perspective on life, they should be done in small doses and very sparingly in a year. These drugs can be useful for the creator, but are really not something I recommend doing very regularly. Also, only normally with good friends/people you can trust.

Alcohol:

I have finally reached an age where I realise why alcohol is legal. It is the drug that affects us the least, in small quantities. Assuming we are not drinking huge amounts, it can have a small effect the day after and then it is gone. Of course, I am not talking about those who binge drink, I am talking about someone who is drinking within the government's recommended weekly amounts. So, after a gig it can be great, but I would argue it is not going to make you any more creative! Again if you are using it because you are nervous pre-gig, of course one or two can 'oil the wheels' and, essentially, what it is doing is shutting down the conscious mind so the subconscious mind leads and you flow more. BUT, this will only be the case with one or two – after that you will enter the zone of actually being drunk. If you are using quite a lot of drink before a show then this is probably because of nerves, and I would recommend a short Zone Technique session instead of alcohol!

Cigarettes:

Believe it or not, they suck the life out of you – they do! If you stop smoking you will have much more energy, you will play your instrument better, you will sing better, in fact, you will do everything better because they really do suck the life out of you. Cigarettes are very expensive nowadays and they don't even give you anything! All they give you is the feeling of the nicotine that you need, because you are addicted to nicotine! So, stop yourself being addicted to nicotine; that doesn't mean going to buy one of those vape things and replacing one nicotine delivery system for another, especially when you need one million adapters and to cart a whole

> *Any drugs I have not mentioned here are just not worth even experimenting with, i.e. they are far too dangerous...*

bag around with you just to carry it! That means stopping smoking and not being reliant on it, because, as I said at the beginning of this paragraph, you do not need it because cigarettes will suck the life out of you.

After exploring the Zone Technique, the techniques I have given you, think about this... what if smoking makes us feel better because not only is it curing our nicotine addiction, but it also mimics the act of Zone Technique, i.e. breathing in and out! So, instead of going outside with your smoker friends and smoking (breathing in and out), why don't you either go out with your friends and concentrate on your breathing while they are smoking, or even stay sitting and just use the Zone Technique for five minutes. I can tell you now who is going to feel better (and it isn't the smokers).

ZONE TECHNIQUE REMINDER:

- **Sit comfortably, close your eyes**
- **Concentrate on one thing only – observe breath or visualising/observing an area of the body**
- **Do not try and change it, just observe it without doing anything**
- **Check that your breathing is regular and deep**
- **Continue this for 10-20 mins**

Now, I have heard a common argument for smoking and that it is the reason why it is a time-honoured ritual in ancient tribal communities. There are some properties that actually awaken creative parts of the brain. I know there are writers that smoke and write and to be honest, I do smoke a bit; there is something about tobacco. I tend to only smoke natural tobaccos and do not smoke daily. As I have made clear, I am not here to tell you how to live, I am here to help you create awareness around what you do and why you do it. Perhaps, after you understand your reasons, then you can make adjustments to your life that will help to make you happy. When I do smoke, I think about it. If I am unhappy about smoking, I don't smoke! I don't use the tobacco to cure anxiety or make me happy. Please think about why you are smoking and if you smoke more than a few cigarettes a day, just ask yourself why you do that and try and be honest and understand what is happening.

Any drugs I have not mentioned here are just not worth even experimenting with, i.e. they are far too dangerous, addictive and a waste of time (speed being one of them, unless you really want to stay up for a long time!). There is no discussion about whether they will increase your creativity or not, I will just say "NO!", don't bother!

If you want to give cigarettes up, then I can highly recommend Allen Carr's book, *Easy Way To Stop Smoking* (Arcturus Publishing Limited, UK 1985).

Before you do any drugs, it would be great to ask yourself whether you are acting out of FEAR or LOVE! Meaning: a) are you trying to cover a deficiency, in which case is there another way to cover that deficiency, or b) are doing it out of curiosity, or c) because you want to LOVE and you are happy and just in your flow. I would argue that the latter is less likely, although if you are focused to learn and want to see different perspectives then, of course, it is entirely possible you are in the space where this experience may benefit you. I invite you, before partaking in drugs, to use the Zone Technique for 10-15 minutes and decide afterwards whether you are doing this out of fear or love. If you are doing this out of fear, i.e. you are nervous and you want to unlock this creative energy – whatever it is you're scared of – then I would suggest that you should be using the Zone Technique instead and thinking about other things. If you want to do it because you love psychedelics and because you are a mischievous adventurer, then enjoy it but enjoy in moderation.

In terms of helping your creations, drugs *can* offer you inspiration and perhaps you'll even create while you are high. I would not recommend any of them as a tool to fuel creation on a regular basis. It may assist you in taking you out of your head and into a 'higher' realm. There is a phrase that comes to mind right now: *if you have to use drugs to get yourself to work, then you have big problems!* Remember, you will also have comedowns to deal with, which again may fuel your creativity. The danger of this up and down approach is that other parts of your life may become unstable through drug use. So you must have your eye on the consequences for your overall existence and, in turn, those on your musical career.

One thing I would say is that if you are using this tool, your band needs to be very, very careful about the frequency, because I can tell you now – absolutely and categorically – that if you are doing these things regularly, you are exactly on the spectrum of acting dysfunctionally and can affect the dynamic to a point that can be extremely detrimental to your mental state, the band's health and your dynamic as a group of people who are trying to achieve something that has been tried by millions who have failed before. This means one thing is for sure, you need your edge, you need your power, and the majority of the time you are working together you need to be in your true power, your best self, which is bound to be diminished by drugs.

Have you ever been on a long run or lifted some weights?

Well I would argue that going for a run, lifting weights and anything like that, as well as the Zone Technique, is going to be a hundred million times better than doing drugs. Of course, not as much fun and yes, you should have fun and yes, you should do these things, but please, please, please, understand that there is a very short distance between fun and destructiveness (f***ing everything up), and believe me when I tell you, I have been to that place – yes, too many times – it is not a nice place to be and it renders the fun obsolete.

If you have reached this point of the chapter and you feel you want to, once and for all, get out of the habit of drinking, drugs and smoking, then I have a challenge for you should you wish to accept. Of course, there are different theories, but ancient wisdom suggests that it takes 21 times of facing a challenge to break a habit. There is a common misconception, which I myself have been involved in, which is: if I am not drinking, smoking, or doing drugs I should avoid the party. It is what people who have addiction problems do, of course. If you are hanging out with addicts only and you wish to give up a substance, then get away from them! But if you are hanging out with recreational users of any of these substances and wish to give up, I give you this challenge. Go out to those places sober 21 times! Yes! Go to the pub, club, rehearsals, wherever it is that you 'use' and tick them off 21 times, and I think you will have formed a new habit. Then I can suggest that you may well be able to go for a fun club night where you get high, but you will be able to resort back to a sober life and you would have proven to yourself that you don't need any of the substances listed in this chapter. Try it! It definitely works. As you have a goal and an aim, it makes it easier. You may even be relieved that you don't have all this extra stuff to worry about – scoring drugs, carrying tobacco and filters and lighters, and of course the financial benefits can be remarkable, you'll need a lot less money to go and have fun, next to nothing really! You will also find that as people are getting loaded around you, you actually buzz off of their energy and as they lose their inhibitions you will lose yours too! Be cautious, look outside your head when someone offers you something, and concentrate on your breathing. Zone in on the chat, the dancing, everything else that is going on besides the consumption! Be happy breathing, talking, dancing and really focus on all the positives going on around you. Then be smug and feel happy, in the next few days, when you feel like gold and everyone else is feeling ropey and remember that could have been you.

At first, when you give up any of these things, life may seem empty like there is a void. Maybe you'll even think, *Well what else is there without these things!* because any time you have felt uncomfortable, you have turned to any one of these as a form of escape, or a crutch to lean on.

> It's so easy to jump into the pattern of just going back to the drug, ciggy, alcohol, whatever...

This period of empty feelings can last several weeks. After that time you will start finding different things interesting. There'll be little tiny sparks at the beginning, and if you put strategies in place to plan for different activities to the ones you are used to, for a few weeks, as a distraction, while your body and mind are dealing with this withdrawal stage, it will help a lot.

Avoid your usual behaviours with the usual people (so you may end up hibernating a bit, which is fine!), then after another few weeks you'll start seeing a difference in your thinking. Of course it's not the same for all of us, but you will probably notice yourself becoming interested in loads of other things. Remember, we are humans and we are adaptable creatures. It just takes time to acknowledge the change. A mini evolution if you like!

Eventually, and I mean after some serious weeks (which are bound to be challenging, but you can do this…), you will realise that the whole time you were focused on drugs, drink and escape there was all this other stuff that you may have been, or are actually, interested in doing with your time. The problem is that a lot of those habits draw you away from thoughts of other things. It's so easy to jump into the pattern of just going back to the drug, ciggy, alcohol, whatever your vices are. They dull your senses and so you perceive lots of things to not be of interest, too out of reach, too difficult, when actually they are, you just can't appreciate them in your dulled state.

I have seen the results of both a thousand times over. People who were addicted to certain behaviours and, after giving them up, take stock and act in a healthy manner, have opened up so many possibilities around them, it's astounding watching real transformation. I have a great deal of experience of this. Check yourself and your habits! Open up new worlds. Give it all a go for an extended period, like some months, and really commit to a change and you will see results that make you want to be more controlled when it comes to these substances.

It's a cliché, but I will say it anyway, when you are getting high YOU think you're high, but you may well be low (depending on the drug and the motivations for doing that drug).

Drugs skew your judgement which can sometimes be a good thing, if you are in your head a lot about annoying stuff and giving yourself a hard time. However, they can offer inspiration and help you to access a different plane of thinking. Therefore, whilst on drugs, it's a good time to try out and think of new ideas. I always write notes about things I think are really great ideas when I am high. Unfortunately, in the cold light of day, most of them when I look back are fanciful or shite. But some are gold. As long as you know the gold may be there, but you must wait for sobriety and to feel happy and content before making those decisions. The number of times I have written to people, sent voice notes, etc. and realised that it only felt exactly right because I was on drugs are too many to count. SO JUST PAUSE, with enjoyment and pleasure, film things, think of ideas, write notes and plan, and then look at everything again with a fresh pair of eyes when you are not HIGH!

The other advice I have IF you are going to do drugs is to approach your drug use more scientifically and spiritually, rather than for hedonistic escape (though that can be fun and you may learn some stuff). I think using drugs to get deep, talk, or explore is a better reason to take them. I have even jammed many times on drugs and it's exceptionally fun and different sometimes, the magic happens, so it's worth recording it on a phone or something. BUT I would not do a gig on drugs, I argue it would never be as good as when you are in the zone in a natural state. A lot of the time it is fun to jam on drugs, but you end up playing quite a lot shitter than you normally would! There may well be some odd bit of gold and some interesting ideas that come up though. Of course there are exceptions, but I would say a general rule is to take drugs sensibly, add a sprinkling of silliness in a safe environment with people that you truly connect with and use their powers of flow, fresh perspectives, amazing chat and true new findings that you can bring into your life and creations.

Particularly when taking psychedelics, I can access what I feel is the spiritual realm. A space of no time, where minds merge, almost becoming telepathic with the people around you. I don't do psychedelics in public places and usually within a home setting. Try and make sure everything and everyone is as safe as possible, that you are prepared for the roller-coaster ride and that it will take you wherever it leads. You must relinquish control and be happy to experience the journey.

If you are using drugs to escape, well then you are masking some shit that you better deal with soon because if you are taking drugs to mask it then it is just growing bigger and you are taking yourself to a bad place. You need to STOP and make some serious decisions after a few weeks

> *Try and make sure everything and everyone is as safe as possible, that you are prepared for the roller-coaster ride...*

of sobriety. Notify friends and get some support around you. See my chapter at the end about building a community and setting up a Staying Sane group.

CHAPTER 7

Let it Go, Get Over Yourself and Do Some Personal Development Work!

Facing the Day:

Face your fears in a brave way – challenges will come to you anyway, so, you need to face them; attack and shatter them before they destroy you.

Let's just take the example of sitting at home and deciding you won't go out today because you feel weak and not mentally stable. You get some movies racked up, roll up a reefer and make a cup of tea – it sounds idyllic doesn't it? At various points in the day, you are then plagued by your head telling you: *why aren't you doing anything, you're not achieving, you'll never write again, your career is going to go down the tube, you'll never amount to anything.* Then, in between you enjoying the movie for a short time until your head comes back in with horrible messages that are not really true, then… the doorbell rings.

You jump out of your seat. You don't want visitors, you can't see anyone. After all, you chose not to go out today! So, you hide in the lounge with the movie off, so no one can detect anyone being in. They ring again – your heart rate is up; you are a bundle of nerves. You sense the person has gone. It was a delivery of something you have waited on for ages, and now there is a note on the doormat that says you have to go and get it from the delivery office. You continue to sit 'watching' the movie and make another reefer. Then you get hungry and realise there is no food in the house. You now have a choice, to get dressed and go to the shops, or sit around hungry and a bundle of nerves. Finally, after several hours of procrastination, you are so hungry you decide to go to the local shop which is less that a 10-minute walk away. You don your most casual, almost bed clothes and walk to the shop. You avoid eye contact with people and you are in your head.

Eventually, you get to the shop (your only focus on the way was what you would buy and for how much), you get in, find things, queue, buy and you're out of the shop and on the way home. You already start feeling a little better. You get home and start preparing the food and then eat it. Now you feel much better, you fulfilled a minute challenge in your day and it was your choice, plus, you actually ventured outside and realised that it was not too hostile and was not bad at all! This is a very mundane example but shows how dramatic things can get in your head if you put off facing challenges within your day.

Plan to do something you don't want to do first thing in the morning. Perhaps that could be as small as getting out of bed and putting the rubbish out. It may be going for a 10-minute walk in the cold. It could be having a cold shower, going for a run, or straight to the gym. It could be answering all the emails you have stacked up, OR, dare I say it, perhaps the best of all, use the Zone Technique or try praying and accepting gratitude! The theory being, it will help you to have a great day! Is it fair to say you will face challenges today anyway? If you choose to challenge yourself BEFORE those challenges come, then you will have a much better day, you will give yourself more confidence to face the challenges that come to you, as you faced and succeeded in the voluntary challenge you gave yourself. Now, let's imagine that the first thing you did when you got up, was see a note on your alarm to 'put out the recycling before 10 a.m.'. So, you go to the kitchen, sort the recycling, take it outside and then go for a 5-minute walk around the block, focusing on the beauty of the trees, the sounds of the birds and the people driving to work and being active. You come back and you make a coffee and have a shower; you are ready to face the day.

Gratitude

We have spoken of this earlier, but I want to mention it again in this context. A prayer of gratitude, at any time, is very powerful but in the morning it is especially powerful. Remember the exercise about writing down the things you are grateful for? I cannot recommend this enough. The more the better, I would say, but three is a great start. You can do it from the moment you wake. You can have things written on your wall, on your phone, or by your bed on a pad that you look at. It is as powerful as the Zone Technique to think and focus on how grateful you are. As previously mentioned, the mind is very good at focusing on the negative (creating blocks), if you can possibly direct it towards the positive then, over time, you will help train the brain to keep coming back to those positive thoughts. Decisions you make are so

> *in order to make changes in your life you should start with the small things that are easy to change...*

important, you can change every single behaviour that you want to by making decisions and putting systems in place.

Every decision you make affects the future. In ancient wisdom a spiritual idea exists that in life we have to withstand the battle between the good inclination and the bad inclination that lives within us. Of course, this makes total sense and this is probably a pretty universally accepted idea today. The wisdom goes one stage further though, the idea that if you make a decision from your good inclination, then you are likely to make further decisions from that perspective. Whereas, if you make a decision based on your bad inclination then you are likely to continue to make your next decision from this place. Imagine a fork in the road. The right fork leads you to a place of discipline, productivity and enjoyment of creation. The left leads down a road of mindless hedonism and destruction. Momentum leads down both paths, but momentum to what?

So, the working example is an extreme one (in order to illustrate my point), but probably not that out of the ordinary in consideration of your past actions. With the right fork you have the chance to sit and create new music, work on your website and send off some emails for your career. The left fork is to order some cocaine and see what happens because you are a bit bored and feel uninspired. You decide to do the latter. So once you order some coke, you get quite horny and you then ring your mate's ex who you really fancy. You end up going to the pub together. One thing leads to another and, before you know it, you are back at yours in bed with each other! You enjoy an epic night and so much happens. But when you wake up in the morning, you see that fork in the road so clearly. You see the pathway you chose and you regret it, feel ill and hate yourself for making a terrible decision that has a huge impact. You have created self-loathing, you spent so much money, you feel wretched and, because you feel so bad, instead of doing some exercise you start drinking again. Pretty soon, 3 days have gone by. You still have the dark cloud of dealing with the politics of sleeping with your friend's ex, which is not going to be pretty, and you have been completely unproductive when it comes to all the stuff you needed to do. In order to get out of this funk, and reclaim the 'good' momentum, you need to make some changes.

It is a well-known psychological theory that in order to make changes in your life you should start with the small things that are easy to change. For example, if you have been drinking alcohol for 3 days in a row, then stop drinking. If your room is a complete mess, then tidy it. If you have bills to pay, work to do, then start doing it. Another theory, which I really connect to, is DO THE OPPOSITE. The idea that if your life is a complete mess, and you feel like everything you do just leads down a dark path then, when you make decisions, start deciding on the opposite thing to the decision you would normally make. This can be as easy or as challenging as you make it. You can start to buzz about "doing the opposite..." feeling like you want to score a load of cocaine and deciding NOT TO. This can be as easy as, instead of going to the pub, you use the Zone Technique and then play music. Instead of putting off that thing on your to-do list, you do it immediately!

Just remember that every decision you make NOW will have repercussions for the future. Just as every decision you previously made had an effect on where you are right now. EVERY DECISION. That is kind of heart-warming isn't it? Well, I'll explain. Instead of being completely down about every bad decision you have made and where you are because of them, it means by changing the decisions you make right now you can have a cosmic impact on your life, which you will see take shape within days. You can turn your life around, right now, starting with just ONE good decision. Or we can say you need to make different choices and decisions, just for today, and see where you end up later this week.

Also, remember that right now, in this very moment, you can affect everything that happens next, literally, by making a good decision. This means you should take some time in making a decision. When I say time, I mean a good minute or a few. I have a friend who told me about the 1-minute Zone Technique; it is a great concept. Just take a decision that has to be made and instead of knee-jerk reacting, think about each possible outcome for one minute, stop, breathe and focus on the outcome of one route and then the other. By the time you have finished you have clearly mapped out the possible outcomes of each path. You can then breathe and relax into making a decision that truly feels like the right one.

In order to make the best decisions and create an unstoppable and great momentum, it may feel counter-intuitive, but I say STOP! Just stop and be in the here and now. For the most important decisions you must be completely present, self-aware, focused and the conscious mind needs to be quiet. So use the Zone Technique for a minute. Focus on your breath, feel into the present and feel your body as we have practised. Then think about the potential outcomes that each decision could create.

The delicate situation with art is that you twist and turn and toil in your music and lyrics and, therefore, become married to your creations. You have been in the bubble of creation, you understand your expression and what you are trying to say, because by the time you finish, or have brought it to a point that you are prepared to present it, you have either decided to bin it – because it simply is not good enough – or you like it.

Here begins the issue; how can you make something you really like – a creation about which you have a complete understanding and perspective – and then allow people to 'help' you with it; bringing their ideas on how to 'improve' it? This can happen with bandmates, producers, label execs, promoters, managers, publishers and especially with that 'bloke in a pub' (this is the friendly term I use, for that guy or girl who thinks they know about the music business, because they are a music fan).

My advice in this situation is simple – listen to everyone, nod and take in their opinions. It is not a bad thing to listen to everything, BUT you do not need to act on their advice and certainly, they are not necessarily right. The reason why these people are commenting on your works is because they feel invested for some reason. This should only be taken for what it is, a massive compliment. This is extraordinary in itself, that people are excited enough to have you and your creations in their sphere of conversation, so appreciate it and see it as supportive. You do not need to tell them they are wrong; hear them, pay attention and see what resonates.

So, this is an important point.

Because you are a musician and, as we have discussed, you have been using the Zone Technique from an early age when you started learning your instrument, you are in touch with your feelings – more than the average person I would expect. If you are keeping a regular Zone Technique practice and playing regularly, then you are even more sensitively tuned in.

EXERCISE: Try and observe the place in your body that reacts in anger, stress and frustration. For example, I know from observing the sensations in my own body in deep Zone Technique sessions, that my stress builds up at my solar plexus and in the front of my head. So when I use the Zone Technique, I observe these areas. Firstly, I tune into my breathing and then I start observing the solar plexus; as I observe and concentrate, without trying to change anything, I have complete awareness focused on my solar plexus, 'looking' at it I feel it loosen. As soon as I try and interrupt, make it loosen more quickly, or untwist faster, then I lose the focus and the Zone Technique pattern – I have left 'the zone' momentarily. I acknowledge that and then go back in, just observing and not trying to change anything, acting as an explorer in a new land, constantly analysing the feeling, without changing anything. Acknowledging, *wow I feel my solar plexus untwisting, this is quite cosmic*, I then observe further. I can do the same to my head, my prefrontal cortex, and feel a significant loosening in my head. I have an unfounded, non-medical theory that people often suffer from migraines because they are stressed and hold a lot of stress tension in their heads.

If you are one of these people, why not try this Zone Technique, focusing on those stress areas in your head. Remember, you are not *trying* to release the tension, you are merely observing the tension, without trying to change it. If you maintain focus, like a detective, acknowledging the feelings and accepting the tension, then you will find it will loosen the tension. I cannot guarantee this will help migraines, as I said, it is a non-scientifically proven theory I have!

So, if you get to a place of sensitivity where the above is possible, what is also possible is to then notice when these areas of stress are starting up. Especially notice it when you are in conversation about your latest 'baby'. Your latest creation is so important to you, see how you react when people start giving their opinions to you even, dare I say it, criticisms! Once you have felt those feelings of anger, frustration, or pain, when someone is coming with their criticism, try and understand from where that feeling is coming.

Are you suffering from ego issues? Is this person making sense? What is it about their comments that annoy/anger/ frustrate you? Do you trust this person; is that the issue – lack of trust? That is a valid reason, we have to earn trust, and so, if they have not earned your trust, then I understand that. There are countless other reasons why you may be angry. I will give one more example – your mum always said you were a crap singer; you have worked very hard at singing, but you still doubt yourself regularly. Then someone is telling you the

> ❝ **Try and observe the place in your body that reacts in anger, stress and frustration...**

vocal isn't strong enough. But you are convinced you nailed it in this track. It is for you to unpick whether this is your head just repeating the lines from your mother, or whether you actually believe that this vocal is better. Now, here comes the testing bit for you... You need to understand and create awareness around behaviour that you have built up as defence mechanisms from your past. If you are acting on learned behaviour from your past and reacting to situations using these traits or patterns then, as sure as can be, the outcome is not going to be beneficial to you. More to the point, you may well recognise the outcome and some voice in your head that says, *I knew it! This always happens to me!* Well, may I suggest that 'this always happens' to you, because you are acting out the same patterns over and over again!

Until you identify where these behaviours come from, you will, unfortunately, continue to act out the patterns. We will speak later about positive change, but the most important thing here is to create awareness around your behaviours. I will give you an example from my past.

I was not really able to speak about my childhood at all, as I have mentioned it was unconventional to say the least! I have been given some useful tools, through the medium of varying processes (some of which are even ongoing!). These include, psychotherapy, men's workshops – including shadow work, constellations, visualisations and working with the Jungian archetypes (the ManKind Project: the women's equivalent of this organization and their workshops is known as Woman Within), Vipassana (S. N. Goenka), iEvolve (Concord Institute), Tantra and Sexual Deconditioning workshops (The New Tantra).

I was a very troubled child; I had built up a behaviour

of trusting very few people for protection. As I grew, I was a people pleaser because I was known as the naughty, out of control kid when growing up. I have spent so much time exploring my stories, and how the different parts of me guide me ahead of the higher self, that I can now understand where most of the strong voices I have come from. I understand that I am insecure because I was told I was "not good enough" or was "not reaching my potential". I have learned the confidence to know that everything is up to me and I am a beautiful, powerful human being. But, of course, I doubt myself and have stories coming into play.

I now know much of where these come from and I speak about them and seek advice from a trusted 'wise' person/ friend who I enjoy shared language with and I feel has the knowledge and understanding needed. It is important that you also do the same. It is important that, when someone offers you feedback, you step back from your defensive self, and you step into a position of observation away from your wounded childhood self – the hurt little child inside you who has never been shown enough love and gets hurt when someone 'hurls more hurt at them'. Yes, we all have one of those, the answer is to recognise the little you, bring it out, chat to it and acknowledge that you are not alone! Which means that when someone is criticising you, they also have one of these wounded childhood selves inside them too.

At this very moment, you are actually, counter-intuitively, being given a gift! You are being told that, if you take a particular course of action, you will become a much better person. If you are able to separate the feedback/criticism and when you feel your wounded child, you can observe how that feels, recognise that these are the feelings you felt when you were younger, that they come from your wounded child, and they are telling you how to react (probably the way you know how, which is like you did when you were young). But, if you observe without shrinking into your wounded child, without resorting to defensive/denial behaviour, you will actually grow taller than before. By listening, accepting and *using* the feedback, you will potentially never, or at least rarely, repeat this same pattern of behaviour that has seemingly really annoyed people! That is wonderful isn't it? Finally, you will be *free* of a pattern that you have repeated for years!

> "...being your truth and acting your truth, is to observe the sensations in the body where you hold stress and tension

Can you identify the feeling you get when you *know you* are right? People call it 'a hunch', or 'going with your gut'. For me, I can test this by thinking about making one decision and feeling my body stiffening up, the solar plexus tenses up and my head tightens up and even my stomach knots. I also feel a pang in my stomach, the feeling of NOT doing the thing I know I need to, my stomach starts preparing to give me the stress signs; the feeling of being tapped into your 'gut', let's call it your 'truth sensations'. The easiest way to highlight the feeling of when you are living in your truth, being your truth and acting your truth, is to observe the sensations in the body where you hold stress and tension. Observe when you know for sure you are doing the right thing for you. Then consider how these areas feel when you know for sure that you are *not* doing the right thing. This is a practice that you must develop over time, and perhaps you can see it as a game. To check in with your body when you are feeling certain positive and negative emotions. Also, through the act of the Zone Technique you will also become better at this.

Over time, you will become more and more familiar with these sensations. The more sensitive you get and more into your body you are (through exercise, the Zone Technique and breathing) the better. Remember, as I said earlier, your body's sensations will be where emotions are first activated and then send messages to the brain. So that if you are angry, or nervous, and you are able to locate these feelings *before* they send signals to the brain, then you are ahead of the game and you can take action to calm yourself down. Using Zone Technique, breathing and observation you can acknowledge your feelings quicker than normal, helping to avoid a knee-jerk reaction and an entire mood change.

THE ZONE TECHNIQUE REMINDER:

- **Sit comfortably, close your eyes**
- **Concentrate on one thing only – observe breath or visualising/observing an area of the body**
- **Do not try and change it, just observe it without doing anything**
- **Check that your breathing is regular and deep**
- **Continue this for 10-20 mins**

If you are tapped into your truth sensations, it means that when people come to you with strong opinions, you can feel how they resonate with you in your body. This is an incredibly powerful signal and should be recognised. Once you are able to employ this power, you will start making better decisions for yourself, your creations and your career.

So, this is why I say listen to everyone. Take on board their opinions, and see how your body reacts to them when they are explaining their approach, opinions etc.

Feedback should never be discounted at the point it is being given, because you shut people down and they won't want to speak again. They are offering you a gift; though sometimes it will be a crap gift that you don't want! Sometimes it will contain gold. One of my favourite quotes is from an ancient Hebrew text, *Ethics of the Fathers*, a book of teachings from some old wise men who lived many thousands of years ago…

> "Ben Zoma says: *Who is wise? The one who learns from every person…*
> *Who is brave? The one who subdues his negative inclination…*
> *Who is rich? The one who appreciates what he has…*
> *Who is honoured? The one who gives honour to others…*"

These are great tenets on which to run your career!

Now, let's say, your dear creation is absolutely ripped apart by the record company, publisher, or whoever… Well, you are creative and you create because you have to. (If you don't absolutely have to then I would give up now, because the road is way too hard to be able to succeed!)

Creative juices mean you should always be creating bad and good, therefore, if one creation needs changing, binning, then don't be so tied up in it. LOOK, I am writing this book, I will make sure that ALL the concepts I want to express are in here. But, having met with the editor, publisher etc., they have ideas on how to make it better, without ruining it.

Because they understand what I am trying to say, and they come with fresh eyes, they can bring a fresh perspective, which can work amazingly well. Then you, the reader, have an entirely better experience reading this book. Of course, I must assess that their intentions are true and honest. But, if the publisher said to me, "Brett, it would be more accessible if you expressed this paragraph in the following way..." or "It would be much more exciting to put that sentence at the beginning of the chapter" then I would trust them, because they are professional. If I doubted their motivations and felt, deep down, that they were missing my point, or had ulterior motives to dumb down my creation, then I would say so, but actually, as long as there was a good reason stated, I would listen to the advice unless I could offer a counter argument that I truly believed to be my absolute truth. Believe me, you wouldn't want to have read it before those other interested parties became involved, it needed an awful lot of work!

So, learning to collaborate is a great thing. No one likes working in a team with someone who doesn't want to work in a team. You see? If you are constantly telling everyone that this is your creation and you don't want them to touch it then, before you know it, you will be living in a very lonely world! Even the biggest control freak artists would work with musicians and producers, and allow them to have ideas and some creative input (I am immediately thinking of Prince, his bands, engineers, and Michael Jackson's producers, like Quincy Jones). A great current example of this is

> **❝ ...No one likes working in a team with someone who doesn't want to work in a team.**

Rick Rubin, the astounding producer, who not only produces incredible albums for artists, but also ends up with artists approaching him for bits of advice. He will listen to an entire album and tell an artist to, drop a bridge in that song, or shorten the chorus, they listen and the song becomes a hit!

On the subject of writing and not being so attached, knowing that the next creation is only a day away, and you should refer to Malcolm Gladwell's 10,000 hours theory. It is his belief that we become a master in something – world class – after doing 10,000 hours of that thing. So, that means every time you write a song, you are clocking up more hours, learning more about yourself and the process. This is extremely valuable as you hone your skills and become more adept. Actually the book that he presents this theory in, *Outliers*, is an excellent read and I highly recommend it!

Compromise:

Compromise with other creatives, compromise for your audience and compromise with business people who are prepared to invest in you. Let's be frank, they are keeping you alive. They invest in your art to make it possible for you to make art, sell your art and live from your art. I will make a BIG statement now... THOSE WHO DO NOT COMPROMISE WILL FAIL. Think about it, all relationships are about compromise.

Of course, you can probably cite an example of someone who you think never compromised. But, in fact, I would suggest that, even though you perceive that person did not compromise, they have in some way. It is all relative – for Prince, compromise was having musicians playing on his albums, as he went through a time when, as well as producing, arranging and composing everything, he would play all the instruments. He compromised by having musicians, I believe he created some of his best work with the incredible 'New Power Generation' band and, arguably, those hit records would have not been as good without those musicians.

Any band must compromise with each other. Think about all the examples I gave in the earlier chapter; they could all be boiled down to a lack of compromise. I think that, ultimately, a fair whack of examples of band, business and audience disputes would come about because one, or several parties, would not compromise.

Of course, this does not mean 'giving in' to every demand made, but again, referring back, looking for the third way.

We are not done with this subject, we will be looking at compromise on a deeper level with regards to decision-making, which is a biggie and we will explore some models of decision-making, in a fairer, just manner and how to help not feeling hard done by over decision-making and compromise.

Audience and Commercial Appeal:

Please face the fact that WITHOUT YOUR AUDIENCE, YOU ARE F***ED!

That also means that, without being able to reach your audience and giving yourselves the best chance of this, you do not have a career. Therefore, think very carefully when moving forward.

That was the segue into explaining the relationship between you and your audience. The audience buy your art; they support you through creating your art. You must love and respect your audience.

I have to mention Stevie Wonder again. He is a prolific songwriter and he has been touring the world, recording and writing since his teens, so for over 50 years! It would not be unreasonable to suggest that he may get a bit bored singing 'Superstition' for the millionth time live! I know I got bored of playing it enough times in function bands! So, what if Stevie decided that enough was enough and, for many of these recent tours, he decided to play all of his rare material and none of his hits because he was bored of singing his hits? How do you think the audience would react? Do you think that he knows that his audience want to hear all the hits, or at least as many as possible? I know I did, and I am a muso and probably would have a little more patience than some in the audience had he decided to play only rare material.

The moral of this is, think about your audience, what do they like and want from you in order to keep supporting your shows, buying your records etc.? This is a fine balance, because an artist who panders ONLY to their audience can also become bland and obsolete. Part of the reason why you have fans is because you push the envelope, inspire, say things that people are thinking but don't regularly express, inspire people to understand their feelings, express themselves, dance, sing and celebrate. But, it is a balance. At the two summer gigs I referred to at the beginning of Chapter 5, Stevie played a few of his rarer tunes, spaced out throughout the set, perhaps every few tunes he would throw in a changed version of a tune, a new tune or a new riff, or arrangement. He did just enough to keep things fresh for the band and himself as well as giving the audience exactly what they wanted. All in all, the show was spectacular both times. It is hard to think of an artist who is as good live today and potentially better 50 years later in their career!

Now, there are artists who are deliberately forsaking their audience's wishes. This became quite a popular thing to do in the bebop era, where the likes of Charlie Parker and Miles Davis would perform and turn their backs to the audience. It was also an era where massive drug taking took place and we could argue that the 'real rock 'n' roll' behaviour of bands began. This came from the fact that a lot of these players had begun their careers in the big bands and were playing what they considered to be cheesy music that was too regimented. So, they became the rebels, they had a more punk attitude towards their career, audience and, let's be frank, that was their appeal to their audience. More recently, the punk era did a similar thing.

Whatever initially gets you the attention you feel you deserve should not be ignored.

In the days of the great baroque/classical/romantic period composers there were patrons who would 'keep' the musicians/composers financially. That composer would only get that patronage because they were making music that the people connected to and liked. Of course, it would be a big talking point and quite the status symbol for me to be a patron of Beethoven! However, if my composer/musician was no longer pleasing me and I felt that they were becoming 'full of themselves', self-indulgent and uncaring of me or their audience, I would get to a point where I would want to withdraw my support.

In the music industry we had a spike of about 50 years where the patron model was not as relevant and business was booming. From 78s, the vinyl revolution happened, moving into cassettes and then CDs. This meant that an artist's income streams were abundant. Through the sale of the album/

> *...The business models that artists are using now for fan support are much closer to the patronage system.*

single, the royalties attached to those sales, TV and movie tie-ins, merchandise and, of course, the live shows, there was a lot of money swishing around in the coffers of labels, publishers and promoters. Whether or not the artists were getting a lot of that money was down to how good their management team and lawyers were! BUT, there was A LOT of money in the music industry. Nowadays, as the industry becomes more familiar with new landscapes, the money is definitely increasing again, but it is still massively depleted from where things were in the 70s - 90s. I would argue now that the music business is really no different from any other business that sells products. That nowadays musicians have to think more about getting the attention of a customer in this age of information overload.

Crowdsourcing and inventive ways of getting support from the public have taken shape. The business models that artists are using now for fan support are much closer to the patronage system. (Except where a classical composer would have one patron, artists now have many.)

So, therefore, it is more important than ever to keep in touch with your audience. To ask them questions, to speak about your creations with them and your plans and, to understand from them, what they would like. To have a deep connection with your fans is of paramount importance. There are so many methods of engagement online now, through social media, live streaming TV and countless other ways, that this should be a staple in your life. You should be interacting with your fans online regularly, holding live Q & As, gigs and inviting them into the seemingly more private spaces, like the end of a rehearsal, etc., asking them all the time for their feedback, ideas and why they like what it is you do.

Physical Exercise:

OK, so this is a big one. As a drummer, I was constantly exercising my limbs, muscles and stretching regularly. So, I was accidentally, or shall we say unconsciously, exercising and using the Zone Technique. I was still incredibly dysfunctional, doing lots of drugs and swinging wildly from happy to unhappy, still trying to understand life; how to best run mine and unknowingly travel, learn and practice all the ideas in this book in order to become happy.

When I stopped drumming full time to start the management company, I was 26 and I noticed a big difference in my mood. When I didn't play drums, I was less switched on, focused and happy. I had no idea what I was doing and I joined a gym. I had sporadically exercised for months at a time before this period and could feel that it was good for me. I used a personal trainer to show me the 'ropes' in a gym. After which time, I would 'take my body to exercise'. You see this is a way of motivating yourself to exercise. I know, I know, I am one of the laziest people I know when it comes to physical movement! Except for drumming, which had a point other than moving my body, I would always need a reason, other than not to be fat, to move my body in the first instance! I have most recently gained an interest in callisthenics, which is exercise designed using very little equipment; it is mainly body weight exercise. I have a 4-day-a-week programme, every day is different; upper body, lower body, upper body 2 and core. This means that I don't get bored of the same day in, day out exercise routine. Look up callisthenics on YouTube and try and find a personal trainer that knows about it to set you up with a programme that you can get on with on your own for several months before checking back in.

One of the key ways I motivate myself is by visualising that I am the head of my kingdom, the king if you like. I can send various 'men' out to do my bidding, so for writing this I have sent my magician out. In fact, I am currently 'watching' my magician type these words. I am not doing anything but watching, as I AM THE KING! When I want to go to the gym, I tell my warrior that it is time he went to the gym. The time that I am in the gym, I, the king, am not doing anything, my warrior is doing the gym training! When I come out the gym, I congratulate my warrior for his hard work. I am often surveying the behaviour of my various archetypes and talking to them as the king. These are actually Jungian archetypes and work for men who feel they have a leading male essence; there are different ones for women who feel they have a leading feminine essence. I work with these archetypes as much as I can. As you can imagine, this example is transferable into spheres of your life and, using visualisation and archetypes, is an excellent way of making sure that you are living the best version of yourself, as you are holding to account and checking in with the different attributes that live inside of you.

It is pretty clear now, and has been proven, that the very best forms of exercise are that using your own body weight. Swimming is excellent, as well as well as callisthenics (gymnastic training). It is the best way to build strength in joints and muscles and make you strong in body and mind. You will also find that flexibility increases and, eventually, you'll be able to do things like handstands and gymnastic tricks, which is pretty cool. I highly recommend this and yoga as regular forms of exercise, mixed with 20 minutes of heart-pumping exercise to sweat and get your blood pumping! Seriously, the difference you will feel if you do some form of daily exercise cannot be expressed easily. Other than saying… IT'S life-changing!

So, if you want to know about the benefits of exercise just do a Google search on that. But, I tell you this… people who are depressed are told, as standard, to start exercising. If you feel depressed and do at least 20 minutes' cardiovascular exercise where your heart beats between 130 and 160 bpm then you will feel the benefits of endorphins, dopamine and other 'feel good' chemicals being released by your body.

Water:

I am absolutely militant about drinking water. The recommended amount is purported to be 8 cups a day. I think I probably drink between 6 and up to 8 litres per day, which is probably overdoing it, but I know for sure that it helps keep me healthier and happier. I recommend that you keep properly hydrated all the time. The way you can check this is to make sure your urine is always clear! (Unless you have had food or tablets that change the colour of your urine, you will know!)

Social Media:

I recently listened to the Adam Buxton podcast, which I enjoy immensely. He had Caitlin Moran on as a guest. She is a writer and journalist and she made a very interesting point about social media that I picked up on and believe to be right. Social media is so young, in its infancy. It can be likened to a screaming, crying, angry and frustrated toddler. Until we have had it around much longer, we and it, will not find and settle on the best usage and best practice for our sanity and advantage in the world.

Warning: Football (soccer) analogy coming! Whilst I find very few musicians who actually love football as much as I do, I insist, right now, in using a football example to paint the picture for this topic.

While I write this in late 2017, it is nearly Christmas time and Burnley Football Club (who are a relatively small club compared with many others in the English Premier League) are currently 6th place in the Premier League. This is a huge achievement for such a team. They have beaten some of the biggest teams in the league this season. They beat Chelsea 2-3 away from their home ground, they managed to draw 1-1 against Tottenham Hotspur and Liverpool – games that they would have been tipped to lose – and they have won many other games that leaves them in 6th place in the Premier League. In football, experts normally suggest that however things look in the tables at Christmas is a good indication of how things will look at the end of the season.

> ...a fundamental problem with social media is that people are far more likely to advertise the fine things in their life...

The reason I am using this example is because I was watching an interview with one of the Burnley players a few days ago, and he said that Sean Dyche, their manager, had banned them from using social media. It would be hard to map a correlation between their results and their lack of social media use, but I would suggest it is vital.

I have definitely been limiting my use of social media. Of course, it can be a great tool for promotion and to connect with people. But, I think it can have detrimental effects on mental health. For me, a fundamental problem with social media is that people are far more likely to advertise the fine things in their life, rather than the struggles and pains. People are advertising when they are out and doing interesting things, rather than the night on the sofa or how bad they are feeling after a break-up, or that they feel like their life is so much of a struggle. Therefore, it gives a very skewed flavour of other people's lives. When do you tend to use and look at more social media? Probably when you are alone, bored or don't have plans, as well as to fill time when waiting to do something. If this is the case, then after scrolling through the wall on Facebook, Instagram or Twitter, you may get the impression that everyone else's lives are absolutely brilliant, whilst you mistakenly believe that your life is boring, no one loves you and you are left wondering why everyone else is having the fun? You can be left feeling dejected. It constantly encourages a comparison between yourself and others; that is unhealthy for one big reason. We should be judging ourselves only on our own merits; we should be making a comparison only against ourselves and our ultimate self. The only relevant comparison is measured against how I think I am or am not being *my* ultimate self. Unfortunately, social media does not encourage this and, therefore, time should be limited and a great deal of awareness involved when using it.

I would definitely encourage being disciplined around your social media usage. Try and put a system in place, whereby you limit your social media time to around 30 minutes per day maximum, or even limit it to a couple of days per week. Just think how long you spend dong other activities. My whole body shape changed by going to the gym four times per week for around 1 hour per day. I am now fitter than I have been probably ever in my life. I wanted that, so I spent 1 hour per day on it. What do you want? What is 1 hour per day on social media going to gift you after several months? I believe that the less you use it the better. Not to say it isn't useful, even necessary to a certain extent, but like TV, and any other more passive activities, you will find it useful and more productive to limit your involvement with these things that ultimately do not give you much.

Food/Diet:

This is a huge subject and I am not going to repeat the amazing research that is out there. I will just say the following: WHAT YOU EAT HAS A DIRECT EFFECT ON YOUR MENTAL AND PHYSICAL HEALTH, OBVIOUSLY!

So, I absolutely insist on you making sure you eat food that is actual food. Basically, as soon as food has been through some kind of process or machinery that was invented by humans, then it is probably going to mess you up. TOAST AND BUTTER IS NOT A SUSTAINABLE DIET! In fact, a lot of our bread is prepared with chemicals and unhealthy, fast-acting yeast. Be careful what chemicals you are ingesting into your body.

I personally avoid processed foods, takeaways, and I check that when I am buying food that is not raw that there are no ingredients that have chemical names! My rule is, if it has an ingredient with a chemical name (normally unpronounceable!) it is not food! I imagine that I am eating in a time before we had 'flavourists' and

> **"...Be disciplined and careful about what you eat. It makes a huge difference...**

foodstuffs with long lists of unpronounceable words. The remit of this book does not allow me to actually recommend a particular diet or way of eating, you can figure that out, but I know that our bodies were not made to eat chemicals. Be disciplined and careful about what you eat. It makes a huge difference, which you notice after only a short period, when changing your diet. I try and avoid a lot of carbs, bread, etc., which are very heavy, harder to digest and also end up being turned into huge amounts of sugar when the body digests them. Just think about and seek advice from someone you trust who eats healthily, has a lot of energy and looks healthy!

Sleep:

In 2017 Professor Matthew Walker published the book *Why We Sleep: The New Science of Sleep and Dreams* (Scribner, New York 2017). In brief, he explains that sleep deprivation in our society is an epidemic and affects the health and well-being of our population. He proves through statistics that above healthy eating and exercise, sleep is the *most* important aspect of our daily, healthy lives. He advises that anytime we get less than 8 hours sleep, our brains are actually harming themselves. He cites examples of people that spent their lives sleeping 6 hours or less a night and the fact that in later life they suffer massive health problems, often brain diseases like Alzheimer's. Most interestingly, he proves through various studies that the brain, when awake, is actually undergoing light brain damage and it is not until we sleep that the brain regenerates itself! He recommends that we must have at least 7-9 hours per night. Personally I recommend 9 hours. The best part of what he says and for me, the most poignant, is debunking the phrase 'I'll sleep when I die'. He explains that this phrase is complete nonsense as, if you spend your entire life sleeping 6 hours or less, you are likely to lose a third of your life! So, by sleeping say 9 hours per night, you will improve your life expectancy and quality of life so dramatically that actually it makes much more sense to sleep for 9 hours per night! Isn't this fantastic news by the way! Who does not like sleep? Now you can sleep knowing that it is actually doing you an enormous amount of good and that it is certainly *not* a waste of time!

Vulnerability:

One of my friends runs a male coaching business called 'Get Vulnerable'. When he started the business and told me the name, I concurred it was an excellent name. We have had many conversations about this subject and I have concluded that vulnerability is where the magic happens. Interestingly enough, a 'vulnerary' is a generic term for a drug that is used to heal wounds. Facing our vulnerabilities, admitting we have them and 'outing' them, takes away their power. One of the most powerful thoughts, which we have looked at earlier in the book, is the idea that everyone has challenges and suffering. Once we realise we are not alone, we can feel connected and also love ourselves for who we are. Great comedians, artists, speakers and writers, with whom we connect, often say 'the unsayable'. How many times, have you heard someone say: "he/she says it like it is!" or "It's so good. He/she says what everyone else is thinking!"?

We can look at so many examples to illustrate how admitting our vulnerabilities, in the end, is not only allowing the magic of connection, flow and peace, but also gives others permission to feel comfortable, like they are not alone.

Imagine a very simple example: I spill a cup of tea over the work surface in a friend's house. If I act really embarrassed and try and cover it up, even though everyone noticed, how do you think each of us feels about the situation? I would say – awkward! Extremely awkward! Whereas, what would happen if I start taking the mickey out of myself for being a frail human who spills tea? I could say something like, "sorry I can't be trusted, I just come around here, spill tea everywhere. Just don't give me anything else to hold, no soup or any other liquids for the rest of the night, as I obviously can't be trusted!" All the while, saying this, I have a smile on my face, I am laughing, everyone else is laughing and the mood is jovial. We are all helping to clear it up. Then I say something like "don't anyone else get any ideas about spilling their tea, or you'll be out on your ear". Everyone smiles, laughs, it feels good and from that place, people start cracking jokes and, before we know it, the whole room is laughing and joking. If, however, I had remained embarrassed and got angry at myself, or worse still, tried to cover it up, the room's atmosphere would have turned tense and unwelcoming very quickly. By being prepared to 'out myself' and be vulnerable, I am welcoming a much better mood and, arguably, this is 'where the magic happens'.

> *...If we show our vulnerabilities...and act as humans who have frailties, we will get along in this world so much better.*

Let's look at another example, this time a musical one… How many times have you heard producers, musicians and songwriters, tell the story of a mistake?

My favourite example of this is of Ella Fitzgerald from the record *Ella in Berlin* (1960). She is singing a version of the song 'Mack The Knife' live and completely forgets the lyrics. Instead of stopping, she carries on and makes up the lyrics. It is quite incredible as she begins this section singing "Oh what's the next chorus, to this song?" completely in time, and continues with some comical lyrics, holding the tune and rhythm perfectly. She continues to improvise and then comes in with an impression of Louis Armstrong, who was known for doing his own version of the same song and arguably had popularised the song to audiences across America. Audiences absolutely loved it and *Ella in Berlin*, the album, received two Grammy awards! (Many believe that the record gained so much attention, which led to the Grammys, because of this new and original version of 'Mack The Knife'.)

If we show our vulnerabilities, wear them on our sleeves and act as humans who have frailties, we will get along in this world so much better. Trying to hide behind a wall of perfection never helped anyone in the long run. Imagine how weird the following scenario would be… I liken it to hiding in this manner.

You are going over to a friend's house for a party, and every time a new person arrives they take the vacuum cleaner out to clean up the small amount of dirt brought in by the new arrival. They want a party, but they want the house to remain spotless the whole evening. How weird and unenjoyable would that party be? It would be quite awful indeed.

We want the magic to happen in our daily lives, we want the party atmosphere, the smiles, the jokes, the profundities, but we don't want the mess of showing our true vulnerabilities. It is just not possible to live the greatest life without these being outed. But, just as I suggest that if we challenge ourselves before other challenges come we are better off, then if we admit our vulnerabilities we are also going to feel freer to enjoy our lives and not be hiding our truth from others and ourselves.

Tantra:

For some time now I have been experimenting with the tantric idea of holding sexual power. The theory is that we can use our sexual power in all kinds of ways, not just in intimate situations. I have been practising not having peak orgasms and because of my experience in Zone Technique, I pretty quickly started experiencing full body orgasms, without ejaculation. I am a tantric student, not a teacher, but I can give some overview of the theory. In men, we have a peak orgasm and ejaculate, after ejaculation there are some chemical changes and we lose some sexual energy, which is powerful. Men, if you masturbate regularly then you are depleting sexual energy regularly. That sexual energy can be used in other ways other than lust. It can help energise, focus, make you more confident and strong. Women are often better at having full body orgasms anyway and when masturbating, or having sex, may experience different kinds of orgasms (a more full body experience) and not peak orgasms, though clitoral orgasms are generally peak orgasms for women. In other words, if you are a woman and you just work on clitoral stimulation you are likely to have a peak orgasm and lose some sexual energy and some power.

I know from experience, when I have regular peak orgasms my life force energy is lower, my motivation gets affected, as well as my happiness levels! Really, I think it makes a huge difference to my life experience, confidence and zest for life. I was introduced to tantric masturbation and tantric sex and these have enhanced my life experience enormously. This is not a subject that is talked about in the mainstream very often, but I think it is of huge importance. I am very interested in the effect on mental health. With someone that is struggling to control negative emotion and thought, what happens if they stop having peak orgasm, stop smoking cigarettes and doing drugs; what happens? I think the results would be profound and you would have enormous epiphanies!

I studied with The New Tantra and expect to be continuing to study with them for years to come. The thing that separate The New Tantra (www.thenewtantra.com) from other tantra courses, is their realness with sex in today's society. If you look for talks by Alex Vartman online, you will see that he talks about White Tantra, Green Tantra and Black Tantra. A lot of tantra is based on White Tantra, which is the 'peace out' hippy tantra, beautiful and lovely, but discounts our propensity for the dark, the naughty, the sexual fantasies etc. We need

> *...we all have our naughty sides that we like to explore in the safety of intimacy with people we respect...*

to bear all this in mind. We need to take on board the fact that we all have our naughty sides that we like to explore in the safety of intimacy with people we respect and feel good with. This is healthy and another realisation is that everyone has their 'naughty', sexy side and that is great and to be celebrated.

As an artist you should enjoy exploring the unknown, as we have discussed. How about experimenting with this. As I say, I am not a tantric teacher, but there is enough info out there for you to look at this. Try the 21-day challenge www.21daychallenge.com then look into The New Tantra's first level courses. There are teachers, bodyworkers and advisors out there that can help you in this subject. Out of all the personal development work I have done, this subject is easily as important as all the others!

Bottom line, I highly recommend researching tantric sex, tantric masturbation and doing away with regular peak orgasms, unless you're making babies! For me, it has been life-changing, really.

Mysticism:

I have to talk about my personal mystical beliefs. I feel that without imparting these ideas, I will not have a complete book.

Mysticism has been around as long as thinking humans have. A belief in forces, gods, or nature that are beyond our control. We have ancient texts and all kinds of scriptures, hieroglyphics and symbolism from thousands of years ago, expressing the mystical nature of the universe.

I have reached a point in my mystical learning that I have a very strong belief about the nature of humans, existence, the universe, spiritual powers, and the source and it helps me day by day to keep my head measured.

I don't expect you to believe or follow this, but it can be a beautiful idea to cling to and believe in, especially when you feel that everything is against you. By understanding and using these concepts you can solve a lot of personal crisis. I will strongly state what I believe the nature of our existence is, what I want you to do is feel to see if it resonates with you. If it does, then it is indeed truth for you too. This is NOT religious doctrine, these are mystical teachings, which I have found correspond to every religion, tribe, and ancient peoples. The details may change, but the overall concepts are the same, and I have no idea why this is not really talked about in the mainstream very often.

I believe strongly in reincarnation. I believe that we have chosen to be exactly who we are, we have chosen our bodies, our geographical location of birth, our parents and most importantly the challenges we are to face. This is all arranged by ourselves and our master guides (angels, spirit guides) to help us become better soul essences. When our bodies die, our souls and our consciousness live on in a spirit world. We put ourselves here on earth, which is the harshest place for us to reincarnate. Some of us are young souls, some old. Some have incarnated not just on earth but in many other environments. Currently, we have chosen to be humans on earth. You have arranged with certain members of your soul group to meet up throughout life. You have arranged to meet your soulmate. You still have free will, you still have the ability to make bad decisions, and you have the choice not to deal with life's challenges. The reason why you feel bad, frustrated, fearful or under pressure, is because you should be doing exactly what it is that will make you feel better. But, it's hard!

Yes, it is hard because it is a challenge. However, you have set yourself these fundamental challenges and if you do not rise to them, the effect is depression, a feeling of disappointment in yourself, or frustration and anxiety. Having said that, if you are doing whatever you can be doing to help improve yourself and your life experience then you can be happy that you are in exactly the right place. That is not to say that every time you are anxious or unhappy, fearful or frustrated, you are in the wrong place. No, I would say that these feelings are necessary to help you get to where you need to be. They are also sometimes caused by you being your own harshest critic and being way too hard on yourself. It is a good exercise to try and understand if you are being way too hard on yourself or if you are not achieving what it is you want to. But, of course, everything worthwhile achieving can take time. You may well be on a path that is leading you somewhere but you are three steps away from working out what that is. I read signs from those I know are in my soul group. I explore my feelings, I experiment with the possibilities of different outcomes. If I have fundamental decisions to make I try and tap into feeling whether they are truth or not.

When all is said and done, what if you do make the wrong decision? Well, absolutely nothing bad. It just means you messed up and took a wrong turn. You put yourself here to learn as much as possible. Of course, you will mess certain things up and not succeed. The most important thing is that you put the effort in. But when you really are struggling with doing that, then give yourself a break. The most important ways to be in this reality is being truthful and honest, with yourself and with everyone else. That is all you can do. BUT, it is also beautiful to know you are mainly, exactly where you

> **I strongly advise taking at least 24 hours a week OFF...Hang out with friends, eat nice food and reflect on your week...**

are meant to be right now.

When you feel like you need to make important decisions, treat them with the gravitas they deserve. You can do some psychedelics. BUT then you should have a period with no drugs, exercising, using the Zone Technique, talking to people, writing and feeling where your truth is and tapping into that feeling in your body where you know truth tells its story.

So, if you don't quite achieve everything you set out to in this life, then you can do it again. BUT of course, you would rather achieve as much as possible in this lifetime with the chances available. When I say achieve, I mean, personal growth, knowledge, and becoming a higher, wiser being. Looking for good, truth and refinement. Always striving to become a better human, giving of your talents and gifts to others.

If you would like to explore these ideas further you can start with the teachings of Dr. Brian Weiss in the book *Many Lives, Many Masters* and *Miracles Happen*, and those of Dr. Michael Newton in *Journey of Souls* and *Destiny of Souls*.

Stopping:

I strongly advise taking at least 24 hours a week OFF. Yes, that's right, completely OFF. Stop emailing people, stop social media, stop writing songs, stop playing your instrument. Hang out with friends, eat nice food and reflect on your week. Here is my take on the manifestation of stopping that appears in the creative process and is a metaphor for our day-to-day lives: nothing is complete until we stop. Think of the painting, the dance, the music. Once we stop and it is complete, we can reflect. Because we stop, we have completed, we can allow ourselves to fully reflect and see the beauty and all the flaws. Once we have done this we can begin again. Without this STOP we are in a continuous cycle which does not give us time or headspace to take stock and enjoy the beauty of our creation. The space that is created holds cosmic power. You may try and excuse yourself by saying you don't have time to do that. But it is not true, because by stopping, space is created and from the space lots will be born in the new week.

Try it, what you will find is lots of things happen when you stop and you can use the power of that reflection period to begin again in newness. Allowing yourself a fresh start EVERY week!

Intimate Relationships:

Don't start looking for the perfect relationship until you are completely satisfied that you are living your potential and you are doing everything you need to be doing, or at least have a plan that you know when these processes are starting. No 'BS' here. No "I am going to start this" at a particular time. If you know you will, great. If not, you will know deep down that you are lacking truth with yourself and that is not going to help you at all.

Make sure that everything in your life is moving in the right direction, that you're moving towards your greatest potential if you're not living it right now.

If you do not do this and you fall for someone who falls in love with you, when you are *not* reaching your potential, you will see the holes in this relationship. You may not know why it is happening, but, when that person expresses

> *Get out there and play as much as possible, create/write as much as possible. Anywhere, any time...*

an opinion, especially about you, most likely you will dismiss it as nonsense. If they are telling you how great you are, when you know deep down you are missing the mark, you will have little respect for them. You will think, *you don't know what you're talking about, you don't get me.* There will always be a gap between your true opinions of yourself and theirs, and you will rarely respect their opinions. If you are not happy in yourself and you are not reaching your true potential, you are unlikely to be in a happy relationship AND if you know this and are fortunate enough to be single at this point, then go work on yourself and make yourself the best you can be, and you will more likely meet the partner of your dreams when you're ready.

If you fall in love with someone who sees your full potential and sees you living it, you will see that that person loves you for who you are when you're being your best self and therefore would encourage you to be your best self as much as possible. But you will also buy into their opinions and know that they are speaking truth.

The other thing I would suggest is, when you feel you are being your full potential and you would like to meet a partner, write a list of attributes that you want in a partner and ask the universe passionately, out loud, to bring this person to you!

Work at Your Art!

It needs repeating…! Malcolm Gladwell's 10,000-hours theory from his famous book *Outliers* WORKS! If you want to be good at something, then you need to spend as much time as possible doing it. Try and clock up 10,000 hours. If you do 6 hours a day it takes 5 years, if you do 3 hours a day it's 10 years. Just put the hours in. WORK. If you see where you want to be, you can't dream yourself there. You get yourself there simply by putting the hours in. Technically, if you don't know where you should be focusing then you need to ask people. The bottom line though is gigging as much as possible, by playing live as much as possible, where you need to focus and what hours you put in on everything else will become clear. Get out there and play as much as possible, create/write as much as possible. Anywhere, any time.

CHAPTER 8

Momentum and Decision-Making

There is nothing worse than being in a band in which almost everyone is in agreement but one or two members are holding back, or need convincing. I know the waters of the music industry are torrid and need navigating. I know that you need to make sure you are not entering into a bad deal and, if there is a lot of money or your rights involved, you need to be careful. BUT, in the independent music world, and even some sections of the major label world, there are a lot of good people who have struggled themselves, invested their own money and are simply passionate about supporting new music.

I know we would all like to live in a perfect world where everyone agrees. But a straight 'majority rule' democracy system does not usually work in bands. It holds everyone back and makes decision-making seem dismissive to those who don't agree. You should compartmentalise people's skills and have one or two members take care of the business and, therefore, trust them to guide business decisions.

If someone is doing most of the 'management/booking' work, they have their eye on this stuff and understand it more than any other. Of course, everyone can make mistakes and bad decisions and, unfortunately, there will be some of these. However, on the whole, it is going to be better to trust the person/people who have their head in the business to at least give the strongest views for and against moving the organisation into a particular space. If you try to micromanage, then you will demotivate people and also create a lack of trust in that person, which will not help their confidence. You can do feedback sessions with them, where they present their work and their thinking. You may then enter into a discussion which involves the decision-making processes below.

The most effective approach to making a band work is to judge everyone on their own merits. That means, using people's strengths and recognising their weaknesses and thinking about how to make weaknesses into strengths, which involves creative thinking. After around 7 years of being in Def Leppard, their drummer lost his arm caused by a car a crash. On first glance this was a severe weakness and certainly a reason to start looking for replacements. However, with the support of the band, he helped design a kit that he could play with extra pedals and drummed with one arm. Isn't it interesting that from this point onwards the band enjoyed their biggest commercial successes and became a household name. If you are going to progress then you need to be honest, with yourselves and each other, about the skills that you each possess and how you can turn weakness into strengths.

> **You should compartmentalise people's skills and have one or two members take care of the business...**

Majority vs. Consensus:

We are all familiar with majority decision-making: a gig comes in and someone explains the opportunity, hopefully putting forward the arguments for and against. Three out of the five members of the band want to do the gig. The two who don't want to do the gig have their reasons; it would be a 6-hour around trip and they would have to miss a day of work. By the time costs have been taken into account, no one will make more than £30 each AND, what's more, there may be less than 100 people there. So, there will be hundreds of pounds of losses and everyone will be falling asleep at work or may not even make it to other commitments the day after. But, three members think that it is a good gig and worth doing because it would help to start to build numbers up in that area. It's a good club and "we want to get in with them". After the vote, based on the numbers, the gig gets booked in.

So, what happens to the two who voted against the gig? What happens to their feelings? Is that gig day going to be awful? Certainly, these two are going to be carrying some weight and we should be dealing with those feelings. Majority decision-making can feel competitive and dismissive. That is why I recommend consensus decision-making.

Consensus decision-making is not a magic way of ending all disagreement. What it does is to take on board that there may never be full agreement, but there is an appreciation for the fact that, for the greater good, the community, the band, the organisation, 'I' am willing to take a hit and give my consent to a plan.

A consensus agreement, based on the example above, should look something like this. You should nominate a person who is strongly 'For' doing the gig and someone who is strongly 'Against'. Each member states their case, while there's no talking from others; give them the space. As well as highlighting the personal loss or gain to individuals, it is much more important within these 'pitches' that there should be clear reasons why there are advantages or disadvantages for the group/band/organisation as a whole. You can then hold a discussion based on ANY concerns that any of the group have around the circumstances. The group should work to find any possible solutions to any problems raised.

So, Dave may disagree because he will have to travel back from his half day at work to get his stuff, then get on over to where the van will be, pick that up and then pick up everyone else. Perhaps you can all find a way of lightening Dave's load and making the day less stressful for him. Within the original proposed action, there is room for all band members to shape the parameters of the proposal. All objections from all members should be discussed and, as far as possible, solutions to all issues faced by any individual should be offered. Therefore, you can address all problems that are coming from any individual and, by the group 'owning' these issues and taking responsibility for the impact of any decision on the individual, it eases the burden of any one person in the group. It really is a most beautiful process and brings you together as a tighter group.

When all the issues have been worked on, to the best ability of the group, then it is time to look at the voting possibilities. Well, hopefully, you have handled each objection and the group has moved towards easing the pain of all individuals. This may even be to a point where there are almost no more objections. Ideally, by the end of this process, you would like to have a unanimous consensus decision.

Meaning, everyone agrees to *allow* the motion as discussed to go ahead. As stated, it is the group giving consent *not* a solid agreement, more a blessing for the greater good. However, if objections do still exist and there is little in the way of extra solutions from this point, then the disagreeing party has the following of three options from which to choose:

Declare Reservations: The members that disagree, give their consent but want to have their reservations recorded, understood and recognised. This may then be drawn on in the future and that person feels heard and respected, as well as recognised for giving consent even with disagreement.

Stand Aside: This is when an individual has a fundamental disagreement with the motion. It is a sign of a strong 'no' vote. Although it is not a vote that stops the motion happening, it should be a springboard into revisiting and modifying the proposed action and trying to deal with the person's objections.

Object: Straight objection by anyone is enough for a motion to be stopped in its tracks. If this happens, then revisiting the parameters of the motion/action and understanding this objection is paramount to the motion being in a state to be passed by the group.

In this process you should include the following framework:

- Limit the option of blocking a motion if it is a fundamental opportunity that will have a detrimental effect on the group's career.
- Give preference to the option of members of the group to 'Stand Aside' rather than block the proposal.
- It is necessary to have a block from two or more people to have a proposal put aside.

- Only accept a block if an alternative proposal or process is suggested by the person/s blocking the motion.
- Limit the number of times that a person can use their block to only a few times in the whole life cycle of the band.

Here is a flow chart of consensus decision-making to use as you are getting used to the process:

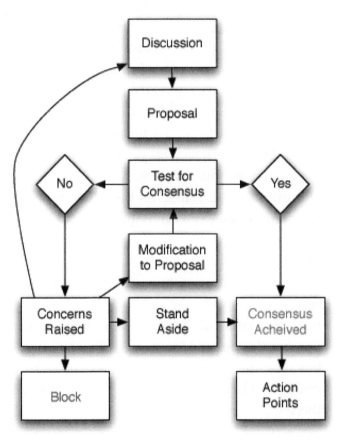

Dual licensing was used for this flow chart on Wikipedia 'Consensus decision-making' GFDL and Creative Commons 2.5

Gig Offers: There is no need to take a ridiculous amount of time over accepting gig offers. You should have a shared calendar where you store all band members' availabilities. You should be organised about where all your correspondence is sent, who is designated to answer it and make quick decisions on offers that come in either from promoters, your booking agent, or manager. Ideally you must accept gig offers within 24 hours. Of course, if certain members are away, then I would put a 3-day cap on the final decision. However, a quick response to any email that comes in with an offer should be responded to, letting the person know that you really appreciate the offer and that you will be back in touch by tomorrow, or no later than two days' time.

> *If you cannot reach quick conclusions and agreements... then you will lose opportunities*

Enthusiasm – Ask yourselves the following questions, be honest and see how you can improve:

- How professional are you to work with?
- How much fun are you to be around, both on and off stage?
- How respectful of people who have given you opportunities are you?
- How aware are you of your behaviour in public?
- Would you like to be spoken to in the way you speak to others?

Yes, I know it sounds like these are your parents speaking to you, but you need to be mindful of this, individually and as a group. Here's some fresh info for you from the inside the music industry:

- People buy from people, meaning you may have an excellent sound and songs, but if you act like idiots and no one wants to work with you, you won't be given any opportunities and you won't reach your full potential.
- Not all the bands that make it are better than others that could have 'made it'. Some will be catapulted forward because as a package, bearing in mind attitude, professionalism, personality AND the music altogether, they are a better bet than 'the others'. Never underestimate the value of your attitude against your musical talent!
- Remember what these people are offering you IS your business, they give you opportunities and they talk to other people. The music industry is a small community and everyone who deals with you has a network that may be able to help you, or ignore you and move on, depending on how you treat them and how great you are to deal with.

General Decision-Making: if you cannot reach quick conclusions and agreements in almost every angle of your career, then you will lose opportunities. This does not mean you need to make a decision the same day or even within 3 days. As a general rule though, you should cap all decisions to be made, as a maximum time, within the week.

Be Precise with Responses and Timing: When dealing with ANYONE in your career you should be precise with your responses and the time that you return with a definite answer. As we have said, gig offers should be responded to very quickly. If you are offered some kind of deal, or other opportunity, you should respond very quickly. Show your appreciation for the interest. Something like this:

"Thanks so much for this interest, we really appreciate it and it gives us a great lift for the project. As there is so much to this, we obviously need time to consider all the angles. However, we appreciate that we are blessed to have been offered this by you and do not wish to lose the momentum and, therefore, promise to return with our decision by this time next week". You should then do as much research on the company, look online, ask people you know, ask business people you know and try and get a professional – preferably someone who you know, or through someone who you know, to help and advise you. You should consider the advice, discuss all angles, the advisor's motives and understand all the information available to you.

I will say this… At the beginning of your career, almost any leg-up is definitely worth considering, even if you had hoped for more/better. There are so many bands out there and nowhere near enough professionals to help them. You should see opportunities that come along as a stepping stone. Of course you must do due diligence into the company and who is offering what, but you should also be realistic. If you have not had people queuing up to help you and one or two people crop up, even friends, at the beginning, don't be snobbish! Don't fall into the trap of holding out for a better deal, as it may never come! The feeling of momentum, of everything improving, of climbing to new levels, can be absolutely invaluable to a new band and even a band that has a lot of experience.

CHAPTER 9

Universal Law vs Accidents

I used to be a victim. I used to look outside of myself, at everyone around me, and often would come back to the same observations: "I wish I was like so-and-so", "Why do they seem to have everything and I am in my situation?", "Why is my life such a mess?"

These kinds of questions only lead to negative answers anyway! You're never going to get a response of "Because I'm actually amazingly talented and GREAT!" out of one of those questions! Negative questions will breed negative responses!

As I have explained, I grew up in difficult circumstances. I was angry and aggressive to anyone who tried to give me advice. Part of my problem was that I had 'trust' issues. I grew up not trusting people, which was a useful tool, because it kept me safe when I needed that protection, but then it started working against me as I was developing through school and life.

Thankfully, I turned to the drums as my only loyal friend. BUT, I discounted almost anything anyone ever told me about anything! I think that made me unapproachable, which meant that anyone who may have given me decent, trusted advice wouldn't. Family would try, but I would completely dismiss them. I honestly think I built up an impenetrable wall that would block people from bothering. Maybe they were scared of the reaction! So, I had very low self-esteem, I was out of shape, I wore thick glasses, I was academically mediocre, just about the only thing going for me, in my mind, was that I played the drums!

Again, during my teenage years, my drumming was also mediocre! So, instead of looking inside at myself and making positive changes (an insight that I was not able to grasp until later on) I used to blame everyone and everything around me. The biggest lesson, that has taken me the longest to learn in life, is that we can make the positive changes ourselves which can completely transform our own lives. If there is an attribute in ourselves that we hate, how can we change it? Well, the first step is ALWAYS awareness. Once aware of that attribute, we are able to ask some deep questions:

- Why don't I like that attribute?
- What does it cause me to do?
- In what way does it make me act?
- Where do I think it comes from? Where did I develop it and what was the reason that it *was* useful?

Following that, I would ask:

- How would I change that?
- Can I change it on my own?
- Do I need help from someone?

One of the bravest things we can do is ask someone to step in and help. Good people want to help others; most of the people you know are good people. This is one of my universal laws; most people are good and inside,

> **The lesson that has taken me the longest to learn in life, is that we can make the positive changes ourselves...**

have a good essence – but sometimes we just get lost in our challenges. Which, in turn, brings up all the self-doubt, self-loathing and lack of interest in others.

I had an issue for many years that I have managed to cure myself. Here goes... I liked sleep WAY TOO MUCH. It comes from being depressed, insecure and an escapist. I would sleep for as much as 15 hours per day. When I say sleep, I mean, wake up, roll over and go back to sleep again. I did this for years and years. Actually, much of the time I would engage myself in lucid dreaming, I could wake up in a dream state and then decide where to take the dream next. Unfortunately, these dreams were often extremely dark. This was kind of addictive and it still happens from time to time. When I would eventually get out of bed, I hated myself for it, it affected my entire life; it meant that when I did eventually get out of bed, I was hiding quite a bit from the world because I felt guilty about these long sleeps and I was surrounded by people's productivity. Seeing people achieving greatness all around me, that first few hours of being awake, was always horrible. I would often then be up for a normal amount of time, but it would be when people were starting to have fun and wind down from the day, which meant for years I was literally a hedonist.

> *You, however, have your own battles, and once you appreciate they are yours, you can appreciate them as gifts...*

I started limiting the amount of time that I would allow myself to sleep. So, knowing that I wouldn't comfortably be able to get up until 1 or 2 p.m, I would make sure that I wasn't going to bed until 6 am. in the morning. I managed to start shaving minutes and then hours off of my sleep. Eventually, I trained myself to get up after only a few hours' sleep, so I could change my sleep cycle to sleeping more 'normal' hours.

I was also told a beautiful phrase by a good friend, which lies in ancient, wise scriptures: "Wake up like a lion, run away like a deer." As you wake up, almost raw with excitement, jump out of bed and run as quickly as possible.

It is really quite hard to do, but I was absolutely SHOCKED at what a difference to my life jumping out of bed would do for me. WOW! It really transforms the attitude to the day. It's almost like the body plays tricks on the mind. So, here are examples of how I think universal law is at play and can affect your entire day.

Just as a seed grows into a tree and eventually it produces a delicious fruit. The nature of that fruit is determined by how it grows from that initial delicate seed. The part of the day when you awake is a seed, which has the potential to grow into such a tasty treat. How often have you had one of those crazy, productive days, when you can hardly imagine what you achieved since you awoke that morning, which now seems like days ago? The more I believe in my power, the more those days are happening, every day of my life, and that is MAGIC, but yes, see the very first part of your day as the seed of your day.

I have another theory concerning the start of the day: *do something you really don't want to do!*

As mentioned before, every day is a challenge, right? You can spend the whole day trying to avoid a challenge but, even if you do that, you're bound to be challenged, somehow. You can lock yourself in your room with loads of weed and food and booze and a computer. You watch loads of films, smoke, drink and eat, refusing to be challenged by the day. Then guess what? You start feeling really depressed, anxious and worried that you are not achieving anything! That's the challenge right there!

I have experimented with this a lot and I have come to the conclusion, after trying and testing again and again, that this is a universal law that works. Test yourself, before someone else does. This is because when they do, you'll breeze through with confidence, because you were there first! For me, it includes an early gym session (which, believe me, is the last thing I want to do when I have just got out of bed!) or, an extended Zone Technique session, praying from the heart, or going out for a walk within minutes of waking, or attacking the work day and starting with a task that I don't want to do! – Yes, any manner of ways. In fact, the less you 'feel' like it, the better the challenge will be for your day. It will make you strong in the mind and give you the capacity to handle more challenges.

As soon as you are looking at others with jealous eyes, you are wasting valuable energy; you are spending your life force on a futile mission.

Everyone has their own personal battles. The person

you're looking at has his/her battles to contend with and you're simply seeing things that are not a part of their personal challenges, but guaranteed they have a host of other battles, which unless they share with you, it is impossible to know, given that you can't see inside their head and know what they are thinking!

You, however, have your own battles, and once you appreciate they are *yours*, you can appreciate them as gifts that are there for you only to overcome.

It is my belief that the universe is made up of one giant consciousness that has made it its goal to experience every facet possible of existence, every facet of feeling, emotion, learning and growth, for the benefit of that consciousness to evolve. To do that it has created individuals to experience different ways to encounter unique emotions through individual challenges.

Therefore, one person has one challenge and gives the universe the gift of their experience, their challenges, thoughts and feelings. But you have another gift and your unique challenges, emotions and experiences to contribute to the universal consciousness.

So you can't take anyone else's challenge, and they can't take yours. It is yours to overcome, and a gift for you only to overcome. If/when you don't deal with the challenges you face, it will keep coming back to you in one or another guise because it is *your* job and *your* challenge. And those who adhere to reincarnation believe that that challenge will stay with you until you (in your next life) deal with it.

The sooner you realise that you are able to change pretty much anything you don't like in your life, the happier and more ready you are to embrace the joy we have available –

especially as you are blessed with a talent for making music! You are one of the lucky ones who feels they have a purpose. OK, you struggle with how you are going to 'make it' or sustain your career, but you have a passion, and half the battle in life is to have a focus and know what you like to do with your time. So, now you have this knowledge and understanding, I invite you to use it with your fullest power.

I strongly believe that there are few accidents in life vs a universal law.

Think about nature: as I learn more about nature, science and spirituality, I see less and less chaos and more patterns. I see how perfectly things slot together. When I watch a David Attenborough documentary on animals and nature, it always blows me away; how perfectly designed are the systems, animals, plants and seas? The natural cycles that exists and the universal laws that exist so vividly are amazing. I argue that we only see chaos when there is a piece of the puzzle missing. When we have a lack of understanding we see chaos. But, the more we understand about a view, perspective, or discipline, the more patterns emerge and, dare I say, we see a universal law that permeates through everything.

I always marvel at literary scholars who manage to paint pictures with metaphors, using stories to create meaning and explanation for some world event that has just occurred. In my opinion, the only reason why this is possible is because of the natural law that permeates across our universe. I now look for the patterns, often speak in metaphors and make those links. It is a joy to see and understand. Some of our greatest art recognises these patterns and represents them within it.

So, does it make sense to you that if you do not play your

instrument you will not get better? If you do not write songs, you will not write better songs. If you lie in bed depressed, and continue to lie in bed depressed, you will get more depressed. If you rehearse loads, you will get better. If you practise all of the tools in this book, you will become stronger. If you work out a lot, you will get muscles. If you eat loads and sit around a lot, you will likely become obese.

Maybe only a few out of a hundred obese people are exceptions and have some issue that forced their weight in either direction. The much bigger (no pun intended!) proportion would be that they weigh a lot because of their diet, frequency of exercise and general lifestyle choices. Of course, there is always the annoying person who eats three meals for dinner including pizza, chips, takeout and doesn't put on weight. (Although as they get older they may well have to adapt or end up succumbing to weight and health issues.) But, mostly, it is a choice. Sometimes, of course, it is a subconscious choice, that the fat people have been comfort eating because of stress, or the thinner person has a poor diet, because they are ignorant about what is good and what is not good for them.

My point is that there is a generic rule here. If you eat loads of carbs, fat, grease, more than three meals a day, plus crisps, chocolate and sweets throughout the day, and do no exercise, it is fairly predictable that, unless you are one of the few exceptions, you are going to put on weight! Similarly, if you exercise regularly, eat balanced meals, not overloading your stomach, being measured and not over drinking, then you're probably going to be a healthy weight.

So, OK, now you're saying WTF has that got to do with staying sane? I agree. It is an example, to point out that –

although there are ALWAYS exceptions – it is mostly a dead cert that if you follow certain rules then you will be just fine.

I mean, you want to be a successful artist, i.e. eat from your art and sustain yourself so you can continue creating with this beautiful gift that you have to give to the world? So, if you care so much about this and you have invested so much of yourself in honing your gift to be who you are, is it sensible to gamble and assume that you are one of the exceptions? Or, is it a more sensible approach, to work hard on developing yourself, stay focused and try and internalise the concepts in this book, as well as committing to learning and growing as a person. How about looking at those who have been very successful before you and seeing that these people were fully committed?

If they did do drugs (again there are exceptions), I can guarantee they went through sustained periods of not doing. Analyse how good their art was when they were known to be off their tits! I think you'll find many of them were terrible when they were actually high. Most of them would get high in between the big shows or before going in the studio, rather than during their big recording sessions. The issue is also that the artists you look up to were living in a very different world, with a very different music industry, so – use extreme caution when trying to justify your dysfunctional living, compared with the life of Freddie Mercury or the seemingly immortal Keith Richards!

> **❝ ...the artists you look up to were living in a very different world, with a very different music industry...**

The people who get through, if you look at the ones who succeed (except for the odd lucky ones with whom we have dealt), have all put in the time and effort. I guarantee you they all have stories and examples in their lives of extreme sacrifice and dedication. BUT not just that, they have probably, subconsciously, followed many of the premises of this book.

The ones who haven't followed any of the rules in this book may have worked really hard at the art, but ended up with unhealthy addictions and/or unhealthy lives and long periods of unhappiness, doubt, paranoia and desperation during their careers.

CHAPTER 10

Taking Responsibility and Appreciating Opportunity

My grandparents grew up sharing an apartment in East London with several family members and lived at a time when doing the washing could take many hours, if not most of a working day! So, when they eventually had a washing machine, they appreciated it and remembered a time when they had nothing. No one had ever suggested that owning anything was their god-given right. They had to create situations and make something out of nothing. They had to use whatever skills they had and put them to good use for society and themselves. They had little time to sit around and wonder what they were going to do with their lives.

Having fought in a war, or like my grandmother who worked hard for the war effort (she worked in a textile factory), they were programmed more towards what they could offer their fellow humans in society, rather than what they could get out of society. So the house, washing machine and car were objects to be appreciated, they were opportunities and they appreciated them wholeheartedly. They could not have imagined being so fortunate to have these tools that would offer them extra time and give them energy to put into other directions. Having a house, car and the time to put into creating made them happy. To have the chance of getting a job, and earning a living, made them extremely happy. They would appreciate every moment of being alive and see opportunity when it arose.

When they had children, they focused their children on getting a good education and either learning a skill/trade, or the lucky ones could pursue academia and become qualified in a profession. Whatever the route, they taught their children to make sure they could earn a living, buy a house, a car, get married and have children. Many of their generation, and my parents' generation, did that. They had children in their early 20s, were career-bound and could buy a house. Divorce rates soared, resulting in many of their children questioning this route of having children at a young age and focusing on buying stuff. We could see that this route had not made the baby boomer generation happy. We watched as our parents had multiple marriages, sadness and, in some cases, a lack of love for their chosen/forced career.

Certainly, this shaped my approach to the future. I had decided before even finishing school that whatever I did for a job it would have to make me happy, as I would be doing it for at least 8 hours a day. I also did not make getting married early in life a priority.

On top of purchasing a house, car and having children, the baby boomers became focused on acquiring stuff. Materialism has now become an extreme pursuit. We now have huge businesses whose job is to rent out storage containers for people to keep all the stuff they have acquired and don't use (this is particularly common in the USA but becoming more popular in the UK and Europe too). It is now common for people to spend $200 per month on storage containers to keep all the stuff they don't use. We throw away more stuff than ever before. We ship electrical waste to China, we dispose of so much and we buy things we don't need on a daily basis.

This consumerist attitude, I believe, stems from our grandparents' generation, but is solidified in the baby boomer generation. Because my grandparents' generation came from nothing and appreciated all the new stuff that they acquired, they taught their children that they would be happy if they acquired stuff, got a 'good job', houses, cars and had children. We have continued on this trajectory and I think it has shaped us politically, in mindset and what we expect from life.

There is now a new generation being born and growing up, a generation removed from anyone in the West who has experienced a war, or is living on the edge, with few possessions and no time to explore hobbies.

Adam Curtis explains in his great documentary, *The Century of the Self* (I believe it is available on YouTube), that prior to the 20th century, the predominant association to identity was that of a citizen belonging to a country or community and how that person is obligated to that community or country. Once advertising, PR and mass manufacture and consumption took hold in the 20th century that attitude shifted. Now a person in the Western world buys stuff in order to define

> **It is now common for people to spend $200 per month on storage containers to keep all the stuff they don't use...**

> *We focus on what we are due, what we should have, what should be given to us, instead of taking responsibility...*

their identity. That is the basis of modern-day advertising and the world in which we have grown up.

Pensions, the UK's NHS, job seekers allowance, were all created after WWII because we needed a social welfare state. But after growing up with it as the norm, now some see it as a right to take as much as they can from the state, RATHER THAN the safety net that it was always intended to be.

My generation, and even more so this new generation, is now claiming what is rightfully ours. We focus on what we are due, what we *should* have, what *should* be given to us, instead of taking *responsibility*.

Let's take an example of the difference between working for months and saving up for something and being given something without putting any work into achieve it. The first example brings a joy of achievement, confidence and a boost to self-esteem. The second brings with it a lack of appreciation and a feeling of entitlement. The problem being that many of us have been given so much, and have struggled so little, that our strength and resilience has been worn down. Of course, some of us may have struggled in society, relative to others in our societies. But, if we look at the less fortunate in our world, how much have they had, relative to those with nothing? Just by the fact that you are reading this book, I assume you have had an education, have been given the opportunity of learning music, have clothing, a bed in a house, food and probably an income.

What is the difference between clearing up our house ourselves, or having a cleaner? Well, coming home to a clean room will have a good effect on our mental state. It feels good looking around a clean room. But, by not going through the process of cleaning it ourselves, the likelihood of keeping it tidy for more than a few days is minimal. Why? Because we have not made the decision ourselves to put things in certain places. We have also not gone through the process of cleaning it, which would bring an understanding of the consequences of having an untidy room. Likewise, if someone were to sign you as an artist and pay for everything you do, after only a year of you trying to become professional, would you take all the opportunities? Would you savour the feeling of that new, clean rehearsal room and recording studio if you had not played in sweaty hellholes for years or tried recording everything yourselves? It is likely that you would have a feeling of entitlement and that would have proliferated through the fact that you had not struggled at all.

Because we have all been given so much, and we have our parents' generation to thank for that, we now have more and more people choosing to become professional musicians. This has grossly increased the competition we are up against and means that it will take longer and longer to break through. That, coupled with the Internet and information overload, means that for those who cannot keep trying for a period of around 10-12 years, it will be unlikely that they will be able to make a living from their art. This means you need a lot of strength and staying

> *You must never think that because you are so great you deserve a leg-up. There are millions of people in your position...*

power to believe, wholeheartedly, in what you do. You must believe that if you don't ever make a living from it, you would still be creating art in one way or another.

Artistry used to be about counterculture, some of the most exciting art ever produced was anti-establishment and formed a protest movement. Where is this art now? Is it really a problem that we are all way too well off and have not truly had the struggles or interesting experiences that make great art?

You must take responsibility for your choices, to be disciplined and not to expect that anyone who gets involved with your project is going to be some kind of magician. You will attract people to your project if you drive it. You must create the momentum, energy and brilliance in order for other people to feel drawn towards it. You must never think that because you are so great you deserve a leg-up. There are millions of people in your position who have decided they wish to be professional musicians. There is nothing worse than pouring immense energy into a project and not being appreciated, or dealing with people who think they are so good that we, as the business people, are lucky to be working with them.

A project is driven by those in the band, the artists themselves. As soon as you take your foot off of the gas, everyone around you will too. This is because the belief has to shine through you. If you are excited, humble, energised and great to be around, you will attract like-minded souls who believe in you and want to help you. Those who feel appreciated and valued will work hard for you. If they see you taking responsibility, then they will too.

I remember Rod Temperton, the great songwriter of many of the tracks on Michael Jackson's *Off The Wall* and

Thriller albums, telling a story. Rod was flown into LA for a weekend in between recording with his band Heatwave. He got to the studio for a recording session of many of his songs. He had gone through the songs with Michael and Quincy Jones who had chosen a few more of Rod's songs for recording the next day. Rod said that Michael Jackson stayed up all night learning the lyrics for the tracks they were recording the next day, so that he could sing them by heart and raise his performance levels. Can you imagine how inspiring that was for the entire crew, musicians and engineers working on those tracks?

Just imagine you have a boss in a job, whenever he sets you a task and you hand it in, he doesn't check it over, feedback always takes weeks and you know that he is completely focused on other things. How does this affect your work rate? How does this affect your attitude? Compare this boss with one who comes over while you are doing the task, you know he/she is busy with other things, but they come to check, read what you have done so far and discuss your choices. The boss then takes time to rewrite some of what you have done and gee you on with encouragement to finish the task. How much more time, thought and dedication will you put into that? How much better will the results be?

Living on the uncomfortable edge is something that is not taught. This would be doing things that no one is pushing us to do but will make us feel good. I looked at the soiled washing piling up in my room before I thought, *shall I?* Then I thought *YES!* It is exactly the kind of thing that I can put off until tomorrow. Have I got so much on that I can't put the washing on and then spend 10 minutes hanging it up in an hour or so? NO! But, I could just as easily leave it until tomorrow. Is it slightly uncomfortable for me to do it right now? Yes! – So then, I will do it now! It's a mundane example and, in the grand scheme of things, a relatively easy task, but then how many times do you have a 'f*** it' attitude to the easy things like that? TRY AND CHANGE THAT, it makes a difference.

Let's give another more specific example... I am in the rehearsal room and we have four tracks to practise. We have done all four, but three of them are sounding passable but a bit ropey. We could all quit, as it is nearly rehearsal finishing time. One of us suggests that we nail the other tunes properly. No one can be bothered. However, one of us is driving the others, and he checks with the studio and reports back that "We can have another 2 hours if we want. That would not affect anyone getting up tomorrow and we can stay".

It is uncomfortable to stay; we would all rather have a beer, go home and curl up on the sofa. However, we decide to have a 10 minute break and all gee each other up, we stay and we nail the three tracks. After 2 hours how does everyone feel? F***ING GREAT! That's how! Really great! We pushed through the uncomfortable feeling, we got through and we achieved above and beyond ourselves. We pushed ourselves, we took responsibility. We found the uncomfortable edge and we got over it. THIS is how you need to be in every challenge you face. This is how you need to approach every aspect of your life. I can guarantee that if you do this in every situation (of course, sometimes we all deserve to relax a bit and have some

> ..do not feel entitled and instead work for what you want. Put the time, effort and commitment into it.

time off), the majority of times you push through and live in your edge, you will see the most remarkable transformation of every aspect of your life. You will be happier, achieve much more and, probably, this will lead on to a successful music career – if you want it to!

Jack Canfield said: "Everything you want is on the other side of FEAR."

So, do not feel entitled and instead work for what you want. Put the time, effort and commitment into it. If you put the time and work in, it may not lead to exactly where you want to be, but I can guarantee it will bring positive results and you will be in a pretty good position.

Flaking Out:

When booking meetings, make sure it is realistic that you can get there for the time you are booking, that there is going to be no issue. Leave yourself plenty of time to get to where you are going. If the place is less than an hour's travel time, I would leave an extra 30 minutes as leeway, especially if you are travelling around a major city. If you are travelling 2 hours or more, then I would leave at least an hour's leeway.

Business people want to know that when they are going to work with an artist, that artist is more driven and going to work harder than anyone else on the project. I don't want to sign an artist that has flaked out of a meeting. I don't want to hear excuses, unless they are morbid, TRUE and real. Otherwise, I want that artist to turn up without a hitch at the allotted time agreed. This will help to give me faith that you are committed to your career like no one else. You are the driver. We are all working with you. By you flaking out of a meeting, the first step on the trust ladder has been broken, which leaves us very little room to have confidence. If we have been working together for a year and we have 20 meetings and you are late or have to cancel one, then we can be reasonable about it. The last thing I want when I am trying to build faith and confidence in you is that you throw it back and show you are unreliable. I am asking myself:

If you can cancel a meeting at short notice with someone who has shown interest and is potentially prepared to invest time and money into your project, then what else are you capable of? Is it possible that I will end up working on a project with this person and, within a couple of years, they run out of steam? Or will they work outside of our deal, or will something else go wrong? What kind of person cancels a meeting with someone that may help them?

Answer: Someone that most music industry people will not want to work with.

Really, because there are loads of other options where I can put my energy. It shows a lack of understanding about the amount of competition there is in this game. So be warned, showing any signs of being unreliable, especially at the beginning of your career, and you are likely to damage your career considerably. We will feel disrespected and feel that you demonstrate a complete lack of understanding of what you need to do to sustain a successful music career. That you don't take yourself or others seriously. So, you have been warned!

DO WHAT YOU SAY YOU ARE GOING TO DO, WHEN YOU SAY YOU WILL DO IT.

Along with this, one of the most powerful things you can do is not to chat too much about something you are going to do.

For example, I only started telling a lot of people about this book once I had written 25,000 words. I then told people outside my close circle of friends when I was closer to 50,000 words, i.e. the book was happening.

A specific music example would be, don't tell people you will be making an album, doing a tour etc. Tell people when you are actually in the studio recording, when you have written a load of songs, or when your tour is actually booked.

I recently watched HBO's series *The Defiant Ones* on Netflix, how Dr. Dre and his friend R&B singer Tyrese Gibson nearly scuppered the Apple buyout of Beats Electronics for over $3 billion. On the weekend the deal was being drawn up, pre-signing, Jimmy Iovine had warned Dre that word of the deal had been leaked on the Thursday and that he needed to keep completely out the way and quiet over the weekend. Dre went to the studio intending to keep a low profile, except that large amounts of alcohol were consumed amongst him and his friends. Before Iovine knew it, he received a phone call informing him that a video was circulating online over the weekend, which was Dre and Tyrese Gibson, talking about 'the first billionaire in hip-hop!'. The deal went through, but this kind of thing could have affected the markets and easily either shaved billions off of the deal, or seen the deal taken off of the table.

CHAPTER 10.5

Fear and Mind Power

Our brains are built in such a way that we are much better at seeing the negative than the positive. Dating back thousands of years, we would have had to live and survive in the wild. Our ability to detect danger would have been the difference between life and death, much more so than nowadays. We have, therefore, grown and developed the ability to spot danger and act on it. This can be seen in our fight or flight response. In this modern age, we do not use that brain function as much now, but it still exists and is a strong mechanism. If we are not using it for survival – and as creative beings – it is not a huge leap to realise that we are probably using that part of the brain, which would normally spot danger, to surmise that we may be in danger, or even create scenarios that may happen in the future that could be dangerous. Can you see how easy it would be to fabricate a dangerous future, full of fantasy and endless possibility, where we are completely doomed and life is not worth living?

It would be the most sensible option to start culling those thoughts. If you catch yourself starting to paint pictures of a future where all is apocalyptic, then I invite you to stop those thoughts and take action to distract the brain using the techniques we have learned about, such as checking in with your breathing, almost militantly!

When that negative voice appears and you are taken aback by it, you are stewing in it, you need to take your focus away from it. This can be as easy as going to chop a salad, playing some chords or using the Zone Technique. Whatever it is you choose to do, you must put your eyes on it, fully focus and fully digest every tiny moment, putting all your focus on 'the other'. Isn't it remarkable that in any situation, if you choose to put your focus on the other and take the focus off of yourself, the mind will shut the hell up!

THE ZONE TECHNIQUE REMINDER:

- **Sit comfortably close your eyes**
- **Concentrate on one thing only – Observe Breath or Visualising/Observing an area of the body**
- **Do not try and change it, just observe it without doing anything**
- **Check that your breathing is regular and deep**
- **Continue this for 10-20 mins**

So your negativity comes from protection. Once you are not in danger of death – being attacked by a ferocious animal, in danger of getting mugged or being fought – there is no point wasting your brain power on worrying about what might happen. The energy you are devoting to fantasising about the future, you could be using for your next great creation.

One interesting illustration of how concentration works to focus the mind was on a BBC documentary, *Employable Me*,[5] about a man with Tourette's syndrome who would spasm uncontrollably and shout obscenities. He had a passion for nature and was seeking employment as a tree surgeon, using a chainsaw at extreme heights! As you can imagine, at first glance this is the last job that would be suitable for him. But, he was given the opportunity to try and due to the fact he was so engaged, focused on the job at hand, he amazingly did not show symptoms of Tourette's and managed to continue employment as a tree surgeon!

I was in bed this morning and my alarm went off, and the first thing I thought of was whether a load of invoices that I sent out had been paid. I was starting to worry about what would happen if no one had paid them. Before I went through 30 minutes of fantasising about how my rent would be late, that I wouldn't have petrol for the car to get to important meetings and a get to gig, I stopped myself. I used the Zone Technique, had a coffee and then opened my computer. One of the invoices had been paid and there were messages telling me when I could expect more payments. I saved myself half an hour of worry and a painful waking up, and I could then spend time thinking about future ideas for an artist with whom I am working.

You are an artist putting yourself on the line. You are a risk-taker; you create best when you live on the edge. You do not need to create that edge by worrying about all the things that may happen, but probably won't. The paradox we live with is that fear is there to stop us getting into danger, although we should not buy into it. But, it can be useful and help us to be productive. There is a very thin line between being engulfed by fear, which will create inertia, using the fear to spot actual, real-life danger and then using the fear to make us productive. Understanding the root of the fear is the trick. Therefore, don't let fear stop you in your tracks, use the fear to create better, more authentic creations. That's why I am insisting that you have a spiritual practice. The fear may get you to use the Zone Technique, after which you are calmer and your mind is clearer to create. Or the fear may make you more productive, because you worry that you don't have as much time as you thought before you run out of money and have to get another job. Whatever fear you are experiencing, try and use it rather than be swallowed by it. Fear has a very important function and that is to motivate us to push forward in our lives, creations and to stop us stagnating. But, if you buy into it and believe your fears, it can also cause inertia and that is not the point of the fear. Fear is to be used as a tool to grow and progress. In this new way of looking at it, fear is a great thing to have, it is your ally; the fear keeps us humble and stops complacency. Fear can help to get you off your behind and get going!

As an artist, you should be captivated with exploring the unknown. The bravest artists are the ones who are prepared to explore the unknown without fear. This is truly freeing and the idea that a human can be truly vulnerable, fight their fear and jump head first into the unknown is what audiences and supporters of your art get excited about. You should be saying the unsayable, exploring the unknowable and delivering your findings through your instrument, voice and creations back to your fans and potential fans. That is your job; that is the excitement of being an artist. You are a social

> *Fear has a very important function and that is to motivate us to push forward in our lives, creations and to stop us stagnating.*

commentator, a superhero, a being who is prepared to live on the edge and, therefore, collect life experiences that few others get the chance to explore.

This is your job, your responsibility and your reason. This is the most incredible responsibility you have. Done right, you will receive immense love and appreciation from those in society who value your explorations and findings. But the greatest feeling of all will come from within; it will be the feeling you get when you are living your truth, BEING your life purpose and doing exactly what you are meant to be doing on this earth.

It is also good to recognise how incredibly resilient we are as humans. Before you say "well, yes, but I AM NOT!" I will tell you to use caution with that perspective! If you are missing your higher self and feeling down, then cast your mind back to a time in your life when you were feeling that these elements were fully present. What will it take you to bring yourself back to that point? What are you currently lacking? How are you helping yourself? Then again, you need to put in place systems to help work yourself out of the fudge. The best thing you can do in this scenario is to start planning the afternoon/evening, today or tomorrow morning. Put into your calendar various systems that we have discussed, like how you will approach how you get up in the morning, such as messages and quotes on your wall that you can see from bed, the Zone Technique, creating, work, what challenges you are going to face, setting yourself realistic and achievable targets, and what things you need to let go of because they are not serving you.

The resilience of the human body and mind to withstand immense pressure and forced pain is incredible. Last night

I was speaking to a good friend of mine who had a baby 8 weeks ago, she and her partner were recounting the 4-day labour that they experienced. They were talking of severe sleep deprivation – he described it as, "having nothing left in the tank. All I could think about was getting to a bed and sleeping for 7 hours!" Then she described the caesarean operation that happened and the following weeks of pain and difficulties suffered.

I think back to the operation I had last summer – it was an operation on my testicles! They sliced me open in four places and stapled me back together again, I was out of action for 6 weeks and in immense pain for much of the time, but actually I got used to it and became stronger and felt stronger afterwards and still do. By overcoming mental and physical challenges we make our minds and bodies stronger. We are able to withstand more pressure from more sides. This is why I advocate physical exercise and pushing the body both in cardio and muscle work. By challenging the body and mind, we can achieve much more. If we cower from challenges, or even stay still and do not develop ourselves, then we will find that negative energy comes to the fore. We can easily get engulfed in negative energy, as mentioned, because of the way our brain works. It is our job to be proactive and fight this by putting in place actions that will bring positive results.

CHAPTER 11

The Importance of Community

What does your community look like? Do you have one? Do you have a group of friends that all know each other and have done for a long while? That is community. It is very important that you have a community of friends who you are willing to allow to call you out on your shit! You must allow your friends to tell you when you are being an idiot! If they do that, you need to ask them why, how and sort your shit out!

Of course, there is the awful scenario that your life is crap because of so many outside forces, that even if you change, there are still horrible external factors that are beyond your control. If this is the case, I would urge you to take a look at *any* area of your life that *is* within your control and start to change that. On the whole, there are lots of things we do that sabotage ourselves and cause ourselves, and the people around us, grief.

You see we are blessed when we are 'called out' about where we are falling short of what we are capable of. Or, perhaps, if our behaviour is simply unacceptable. It is amazing when people know us well, and you invite that help. Just think about how much the people around us can help our happiness and development as humans. If no one actually told you when you were being annoying, then you would continue to be that person.

The blessing is that when we are told that our behaviour is unacceptable in a specific way, we can actually change it. This is invaluable and beautiful; instead of moping, denying or complaining, we have been given an opportunity to change ourselves. "THANK YOU for telling me that I am being an idiot!" What an incredible way to develop ourselves, become better people and change the paradigm we have been swimming in. As hard and as embarrassing as it is to hear, if you see this new information as a blessing, thank the person. Then maybe by asking them how they can see you changing your ways for the better and actually acting on it, you can turn that behaviour into an inspiration to others as well as yourself. It has happened to me, many times! I have been close to crying, or have cried, about it. But, by showing the other person that we are serious about changing, the understanding I have been given, is that the person who is offering the feedback feels vindicated for giving the advice and then turns into support. It is cosmically beautiful.

As an individual, to have a community around you will most likely aid your personal development. It is very hard to 'get away with' stuff when you have a community around you. No doubt, there will be those in the community you admire and there will be those who you despise! This is the value of community. Some of those who you despise will have characteristics that you actually display in your own behaviour when acting from a place of selfishness and ignorance. Those that you admire will display characteristics that you have, or display, when you are being selfless and self-aware.

A Famous Game: select three people you respect and three people you loathe. Note an attribute of each that you respect or loathe respectively. Now look at the next part of the game...

> *...We need to have mirrors held up to us and that is what is happening when you are around others.*

Is there a correlation between the attributes of the people you respect and you when you feel you are reaching your potential? Now, of the people you loathe, what attributes did you choose for them? Is there a correlation between the attributes that you noted for them and a similarity in you when you are acting in a way that you dislike and would rather not?

Your people, your friends and your partners, will act as mirrors to you, they will reflect back at you who you are and sometimes this is painful. Sometimes they will show admiration for you. The point, of these mirrors, is that they will not let you stagnate; they will help you to continue to grow and progress in life. Of course, this discounts the situation of living with total junkies! I can emphasise now that this is not a good idea, as they will not be the people to spur you on, if anything, they will help you build a drug habit and send you on a road to frustration and despair.

I am picturing a community of artists who are driven by art, people who have aims and goals and are following their visions. If you are around artists, as much as possible, who have determination, then this can be a hugely positive thing. It will help you quieten your conscious mind and live more in flow. These people will share in conversations, feedback, swapping ideas, appreciating you, and you appreciating them. This can be such an incredibly nourishing relationship and the more people in the community, the more variety you have to feed off and give to. Investing in a community of artists is a really great way to help you and others in this hard pursuit.

In short, it is absolutely vital that you have people around you and feel involved in a community. It offers accountability and gives you a sense of responsibility – not necessarily in a fear-based way, but can offer you more of a reflection. You can mask yourself and hide from yourself, from your true abilities/potential, because of fear of failure or other fears, but when you are held accountable by standards that people know you are capable of, you can pledge your desires, your fears, your weaknesses to others, who can reflect these back in times of challenge. You will see what you expect of yourself by others reflecting this back at you, then you can progress to being and living up to your potential and when you slip, which is inevitable, then you are helped and held to get back on track – it's all kindness... Especially when you are offering this back to others too.

How to Build Community:

If you feel you don't have community at the moment, I would suggest building a group of 20-40 people whom you would like to join in a community. You can start with a group on Facebook or an email list. Approach people and ask them if they would like to become a community of artists. It can be larger than 40, if you have visions of how that would work, but be warned the admin will be increased. If someone within the group has premises you can use to meet at least once per month, then that would be great. If not, perhaps you can hire a small space and everyone donates a small fee to go to the monthly/fortnightly group. You can arrange sharing groups, which can be run the same as you do the check-ins at band rehearsals: a short version of the Zone Technique, a check-in with one person talking and everyone listening for 2-3 minutes each (this would be a time to know what people are working on and whether anyone in the group sees a synchronicity), then you can make an agenda of things to chat about OR just open it into a free space for people to explore each other's ideas. This should be a place where people can incubate ideas they have, join forces with others and support everyone else's artistic ideas. In a collective you become more powerful, you can share fans, ideas, events and contacts in the industry.

I would advise that this is a priority thing to do. By building a community around your art, you will accelerate your growth as a person, artist and in terms of possibilities.

People have been setting up 'working groups' for decades, to help each other out, build contacts, share information and skills. There are probably a whole host happening in your city right now that you don't know about. But you can build one yourself, in a focused and conscious way, the way you want it.

Looking Outside Ourselves:

We must realise that we have a propensity for procrastination, hedonism and laziness. Living around people who have unhealthy habits can be extremely damaging. You need to be very careful with the people you choose to live with, but living with people is very good for you, as long as they are the right people FOR YOU. Be it a partner, or friends, being around others is healthy and useful. We need to have mirrors held up to us and that is what is happening when you are around others. But also, it is important to have people immediately around who you can be giving and caring towards. If you are easily distracted, like drugs and lack motivation (probably because of your lifestyle!), then do not live with someone who will be sitting around watching TV, smoking dope and partying a lot! You should try and find someone who has a balance with the hedonism and is extremely motivated towards creating.

I put a huge value on empathy and looking outside our heads. The message here is clear... LOOK OUTSIDE OF YOURSELF. I want you to do an exercise:

EXERCISE: Think of someone close to you. Think of their day-to-day life and start thinking immediately about how you could be of service to them. Spend the next few minutes doing that, and then I invite you to plan and create the action you just thought of. If you are with a long-term partner, then dare I say it, this is something you should be doing all the time! If you are not doing it fairly regularly, then perhaps your relationship is not fulfilling! Again, maybe that is because you are caught in a loop of thinking of yourself, about *what can I get out of this?* rather than thinking, *Wow! I could really gift this person something beautiful.* If you start thinking more about what you can do for other people and less about yourself and your needs, well, this is a major step forward in feeling much better all the time.

Look outside yourself when walking in the street, pre-empt that the woman with the buggy may need a lift with

> **I was sitting in my new office, in Camden, London, and a very strong thought of this person came into my head...**

it getting on to the bus, walk outside with your eyes wide open, look at the beautiful nature that surrounds you, the beautiful faces, and consider how you can be of service in every situation. When you are paying for your shopping at the supermarket, how can you help serve the woman behind the checkout? By being smiley and conversational and asking her about her day, and then getting her into a deeper and more real conversation, rather than just a "yeh fine"! You see if you start looking outside yourself and contemplating how you can serve, life becomes much better. Of course, you need to make sure you are doing the things you need to do to genuinely feel good (so that doesn't mean going to score loads of drugs!). I mean, of course, all of the things we have spent so much time on in this book. How much better will life be if you keep training yourself to look outside YOU and put the focus on what you can give others (making sure you are not CONSTANTLY giving at the detriment to yourself)?

A good friend of mine told me of a visualisation that he regularly partakes in and, although unconventional, I wonder what would happen if we all started doing this. When walking in the street, he picks a person on the horizon and focuses on them. He visualises giving them a hug, really giving, this is a 'focus outside of yourself' exercise. Imagine, just focusing your energy on giving platonic, unconditional love to that person. Then as they approach, he says, he has to turn the focus off that as, of course, he doesn't want to make them feel uncomfortable and even feel violated. What is happening here? Why would it make us feel good? Why would it make others feel good? I think it is to do with looking outside of ourselves; as soon as we take the focus away from ourselves, we get outside of our own heads. As well as that, we are focusing on another, which means we are sending thoughts and frequencies to that person. The more we practise this, the better we get.

How many times have you heard that we only use a small percentage of our brain power? It's a tiny percentage!

Well, the theory is that we *are* actually telepathic. We communicate ideas, opinions and feelings through thoughts. I actually tested this once. I was in Australia for work and I was told by a colleague and friend, originally from South Africa, that his South African friend lived in Sydney and that I should look him up, because we would get on. Life on the road can be lonely and any familiar connection, friend of a friend, is welcome, especially if recommended by someone with whom I already had a good connection. I hooked it up and we got on really well. We didn't really keep in touch, but many, many months later I was sitting in my new office, in Camden, London, and a very strong thought of this person came into my head. It was a remarkable feeling because, all of a sudden, I was back in that bar we met in, sipping a beer and chatting. I decided to mark the time and write him an email. I explained the thought and asked him to be absolutely honest, and tell me if he'd had a similar thought to me. He wrote back the next day and we traced our thoughts to within an hour of each other. He had experienced much the same feeling. Imagining being back in the bar and thinking of our time together. Now OK, this is not so scientific, but having spent years believing that we can transmit thoughts and feelings across the world, I truly believe this now. You know it from thinking of someone, ringing them and them answering saying "I was just thinking about you". Better believe it, we are powerful beyond measure and this stuff exists. Therefore, if we go back to visualisations, just imagine how we can visualise giving love to someone, killing the next gig, imagining the audience going mental for our sound, it being the best gig and visualising that we play really well. You will find if you experiment with this and look outside of yourself, this is yet another tool that will help you to feel peace, become successful in your art and enjoy life more fully.

Once you are looking outside yourself, focus on the giving and keep doing that, you will find you start making choices from self-awareness and selflessness rather than your selfish, un-empowered and animalistic self! These choices will always be more productive, more beautiful, more collaborative and have better outcomes than when you are simply focused only on yourself.

You see, you think you need to be about the self, be egotistical, chaotic, live on the edge and be totally self-focused – you then use your art to elevate your own mood and hope that as a by-product it elevates others.

But I am asking what happens if you approach your art with an order, the Zone Technique, mental preparedness, where the mind and chaos chatter are slowed or stopped; that you reflect on periods of chaos from a place of calm; that you step into the unknown with a quiet mind; that you are able, at any time, to step in and out of chaos and when you are in chaos, be fully present in there, knowing that you will, in the future, be fully present in the calm. For me, from what I have seen and experienced, I think this, as an aim for all artists, is a total game changer.

CHAPTER 12

Conflict Resolution

There is always conflict in bands. In my work I often deal with conflict resolution. I enjoy this work, ultimately because I have seen enough conflicts, bands messed up, artists choosing the wrong path etc., and so now I can generally help solve most issues, though if there is a stubborn member this can lead to destruction. I would try and encourage the consensus decision-making process, mediation tools, NVC and other such tools. It is also useful having someone that is not in the band – a non-judgemental figure, who is experienced in band dynamics and can see the problems, almost instantly, after a brief explanation about the issues involved or, at least, exactly which questions to ask to uncover the necessary information, to help everyone see the issues clearly, or even start understanding the solutions.

It should be emphasised here that all conflict should be looked at in a space outside the playing or creating of music. Set up a meeting dedicated to solving your issues away from instruments!

The reason why I have left this to the end of the book is because, hopefully, after reading the whole thing, you have gained useful knowledge and insight, which will help avoid conflict in the future, especially if all of your fellow band members have read it too!

However, I would like to address some themes and elements that contribute to conflict in bands, or with business people, producers and anyone that you may be dealing with in a professional situation.

I find conflict in musical situations so much harder than those in the professional sphere. Why? Because when we are in 'the zone' and making music, we are connecting on a deep, spiritual level. There are no words for that kind of connection, though we can try and define it; possibly equate it with a deep spiritual form of lovemaking? Epic, flowing conversation? The act of pure giving and receiving, without looking to gain: you are just adding your part, your contribution and you are so in flow it is perfect, exactly what is meant to happen. Then conflict comes up about who hasn't been filling in the calendar with their unavailable dates! You have just been offered a gig at Glastonbury and accepted it, based on the info in the calendar. "BLOODY CHRIS, WTF!" Suddenly everyone is so f****ed off with Chris, no one can look him in the eye. Everyone knows that he is an integral part of the band and if he can't make the gig, it is going to be hard to pull someone else in to cover for him. This is at the beginning of the rehearsal, so how the 'expletive, expletive, expletive' are you going to make 'musical love' to each other now?

So, we can liken it to a relationship, where some couples will storm out of a situation like this, in an angry mess, and some couples will actually use it as a springboard into making deep love! Actually, I have been on tantric courses and my teachers have recommended, when there is a disagreement like this, that it is GREAT to reconnect through sex and then try and deal with the disagreement later! Sometimes words are not sufficient anyway and also a lack of connection going into solving an argument, when both parties are maybe very angry, is not a great place from which to work.

I was having a conversation with an artist, just this morning, about his intimate relationship. He felt like he wanted to call it off. He had even made many decisions in his head about this. The conversation we had was profound. We spoke about a past relationship he had had where he had made the decision to break it off, of course without including his partner at the time in the decision. Therefore, when he came to that decision, he had made up his mind and had had much time to think about it. His partner at the time was devastated, and he walked away in pain. He remarked that it took him 10 months, and seeing her several times to talk, in order to start the healing process.

Several years ago, Chris Martin and Gwyneth Paltrow were in the news under the headlines 'Conscious Uncoupling'. At the time I didn't know what that meant, but after some reading and relating it to this work, I feel I have an understanding. It's all about communication. As soon as one person makes a decision, and shuts another out, there will be pain and hurt. I suggested to the artist, who was going through issues, that he open up about them and include his partner in the conversation. Of course, it causes confrontation, pain and hurt. Of course, there will be crying, shouting

> ❝ Because when we are in 'the zone' and making music, we are connecting on a deep, spiritual level...

and anger. But ultimately, by including each other in the conversation and confronting the difficulties, instead of making a decision and running away, everyone will respect each other more. Trying to predict the outcome without having the conversation can be a brutal mistake too. You may be surprised what the other person has to say in response to the struggles you are having within a relationship.

So, back to our studio situation... it is a good idea to have a play of a favourite track, a thing you know that works, which is the musical attraction, and then leave the difficult conversation for after you have connected on a deeper level. Once you have created together and connected, then be prepared to step into this 'difficult', confrontational, disagreement zone and go with an open heart, a willingness to hear the other and feel respect.

Well, as this example with Chris streams out of me, I realise it is the perfect example to say... I AGREE! If a 'business' disagreement comes up in a rehearsal, then perhaps the members who are not emotionally involved can step in and suggest that you use this anger and put it into having an amazing rehearsal, then go to the pub afterwards to discuss the matter, *away* from your instruments. Use the anger, the stress and pent-up energy – perhaps you need to breathe for a few minutes to release some tension and then smash it out through playing the music.

Passive-Aggressive and Miscommunications:

So many arguments in bands, or with bands dealing with people outside their organisation, are caused by a passive-aggressive attitude. The dictionary describes passive-aggressive attitude in the following way:

"passive-aggressive
Adjective;
Of or denoting a type of behaviour or personality
characterised by indirect resistance to the demands
of others and an avoidance of direct confrontation."
(Oxford English Dictionary)

So, let's stick with our example above – it comes up that Chris hasn't actually provided his away days and one of the band has agreed to a Glastonbury show, at which the band cannot play because of Chris being unavailable. When Chris says he is sorry, one member of the band says, "Well, it's OK; it's only like, our biggest opportunity ever!" Another member says, "Hey man, it is such a shame you didn't fill in your dates, we'll just have to see what happens." (With the intention in their head of replacing him for that Glastonbury gig and perhaps for the future!) One other says, "Chris, this is such a let-down, you have really left us in the lurch" (thinking, we are going to have to fire him!).

The straightforward and best approach when dealing with Chris would be something more like this:

"Chris, this is totally f***ed up and unacceptable. Obviously, we are not going to fire you over it, but man,

> **I am just doing this sh*t because no one else does it! So don't f****ing blame me when it goes wrong...**

you need to make sure you ALWAYS put your unavailable dates in the calendar. That goes for ALL OF US, by the way. Anyway, in this situation, I think we desperately need to find someone else to replace you, just for that gig, and if you can help we would appreciate it. You kind of owe us that. You also owe us to not be downhearted by our decision to play the gig. It will help the project in the future, so you will gain out of it. But it is your screw-up, so take the consequences like a big human and know that we are family and we will get through this, with your help!"

Organisation/Disorganisation:

This is linked to the example above; Chris was disorganised and this has led to conflict! I know, it goes without saying, that artists are often disorganised. As I have said earlier, it is the challenge of the musician today that you need to find a way of marrying the business side with creating your art – it is, quite frankly, unavoidable! If you think you cannot do it yourself, then learn! We are humans, we can learn anything! You may be lucky enough to have someone in the band who can do all of this. If you do, then make sure they are being rewarded for it. There is nothing worse than managing a project, as a band member, having to learn on the job and being struck down in flames by band members when things go wrong. "I am not a professional manager! I am just doing this sh*t because no one else does it! So don't f****ing blame me when it goes wrong." If you do have one or two band members who do most of the admin/management side of running the show, you must praise them regularly, appreciate them and PAY them extra from gig money. A manager normally gets 20% commission from gross

> *...manage your project effectively and whoever is doing that should probably be spending at least 8-16 hours per week...*

income (although, if you are a self-releasing, independent band, then you should apply a level of remuneration to the member who deals with each area. See the below lists for potential areas of management that need covering).

You may agree as a band that NO ONE gets ANY money and ALL money is accrued in a band bank account. This can be a great attitude and is a very mature approach. If you are going to agree to this, then I would suggest that you make doubly damn sure that everyone wants this. I would also suggest that you revisit this agreement at least every 6 months (perhaps even 3 months if people tend to be tight on cash in your band!)

You need to manage your project effectively and whoever is doing that should probably be spending at least 8-16 hours per week on it, and more as you rise up the ladder and get more notoriety and recognition. Is that not worth payment? Without them, nothing else works at all!

(20% commission or a wage) Managing and online presence/PR – *maybe outsourced, but the relationship with the PR company still needs managing!*

- *Managing and keeping the momentum going*
- *Networking*
- *Making contacts and building a strategy*
- *Keeping an eye on and driving the organisation forward*
- *Making plans for the future*
- *Making sure all other jobs get done*

(15% commission for each gig) Gig booking:
- *Approach to promoters*
- *Tech specs (can also be included as a tour manager duty)*
- *Dealing with responses*
- *Group diary*
- *Confirming the gig*
- *Booking the supports*
- *Strategy for moving forward*
- *General organisation*
- *Booking rehearsals – making sure everyone agrees to it and knows!*

(A small fee from the gig or perhaps 5% from each gig fee) Tour Management:
- *Routing*
- *Driving*
- *Transport*

(5% production 'points' – a percentage on the record – masters and publishing nowadays) Producer/Engineer:
- *Writing – proper percentage split, based on contribution*
- *Producing/engineering*
- *Recording*

Dealing with artwork, manufacture, signing up to an aggregator, uploading to online streaming and download services, organising video shoots, getting videos online and dealing with PR would normally be worth 50% of the record revenue (not the publishing).

As I said earlier, it may be better to group together the record side, bookings and management roles and see them as a 50% commission from all revenue. That means if these roles are split within the band, you split that 50% revenue accordingly before any wages from gigs are given.

I will not delve any more into this subject, as it is getting off topic, but it is good to have agreements, band agreements and proper paperwork for every area you are managing within your organisation yourselves. You can tinker with percentages, and use the above as a springboard for discussions and agreement.

People Feel Taken Advantage Of/Taken for Granted/ Don't Feel Appreciated:

Classic scenarios, we have dealt with above somewhat. Trying to find the areas where this lack of appreciation happens the most, I would say it is probably in all the scenarios above, particularly when dealing with the organisation/business side, but it can also happen if one person is doing all the writing. Imagine Jim writes 90% of the material for the band and Jim demos all the tracks before bringing them to rehearsals. Of course, there should be a recognition that just because he brings almost finished tracks, if people have ideas, then you should try them out in an organised fashion otherwise Jim may as well be a solo artist.

BUT, imagine if Jim brings his demo and people start slagging it off within a minute of it being played. Jim has spent hours and hours on it! So, appreciate that he has done that. Tell him you appreciate his work, but you either don't connect with it at all OR you can hear loads of ways in which you could contribute. If it is the latter, then again you should

> *...It is my belief that strong arguments have to be made in full, and with passion, in order to be understood fully...*

be praising Jim, because he has brought a tune that you feel good about contributing to. That is a blessing.

Part of this conflict is carried by Jim. For example if, in this situation, Jim feels taken advantage of, then he should say, at the earliest possible time of those feelings, that he has issues and is feeling that way. He should call people to the pub and say, with love and compassion, that he has a real issue and wants to sort it. Do not judge that people are acting in a premeditated fashion. It is completely possible and plausible that no one even realises that they are acting in an offensive way to each other for different reasons, on one side, you have Jim who has done a lot of work. On the other side you have those that are not showing their appreciation and being very opinionated. Both sides need to move towards each other. In this situation, I think it is on the shoulders of those that have not done the work to make it very clear that they love the fact that Jim has done the work. Nothing they say can take that away. Jim needs to hear that and therefore not take any of the feedback personally!

Imagine, for example, that someone is doing all the management and no one gives any plaudits. People don't respond to texts about availability for the next rehearsal or gig and there is a lot of complaining about the organisation, this is going to lead to a lot of resentment from the person doing all the work! Part of the skill and appreciation of being a member of a band or group, which can also be looked upon as a micro community, is that everyone uses their skills to contribute. If everyone contributes in the way they know best, the cogs keep turning, the community, however dysfunctional, continues. This is because, if everyone uses their true skills and brings them to the table then, when someone else is doing the same, you appreciate them for it. Quite simply, you are all leading by example. Now, if someone else has brought their gifts to the table, then it pays to appreciate that, because if you don't show your appreciation, then they may feel that their gifts are not wanted.

What if someone brings unwanted gifts?

Within the sharing groups and the various tools you have been given to work with in this book, there should be frank discussion about the division of labour. It should be made quite clear what is needed and who can do what. You can also use consensus decision-making in each part of a meeting that has been designed specifically to organise who should be doing what, and when it should be done by, for the good of the project.

Decision-Making:

We covered this in a previous chapter, but just briefly and more specifically in respect of conflict resolution, I will say a few things. You need to start from a base of knowing that one of the strengths of working with others is that they may well have an opinion which is different from yours. Having contrary opinions should be looked at as a blessing. The truth often hides somewhere in between two strong arguments. I would, therefore, welcome strong opinions as long as they are given their own space and are fully respected.

It is my belief that strong arguments have to be made in full, and with passion, in order to be understood fully and given their best chance of being communicated properly.

I will give you an example from when I was back in school. I had a drum teacher who ONLY believed in playing traditional grip with the left-handed stick. For non-drummers, you will notice this particularly with jazz drummers. One of the best examples of a traditional grip drummer (in my opinion, the best drummer in the world ever!) is Buddy Rich (search Buddy Rich Big Band on YouTube where you will see a monster, and also recognise the traditional grip). So, my teacher championed traditional grip. But at the time I was into rock, hip-hop and Prince was my favourite artist.

Prince's drummer at the time, Michael Bland, played with the more common matched grip. If my teacher had not been soooo full-on and passionate about traditional grip, there is no way that I would have learned it. If he had not put forward his arguments passionately and succinctly then I would have only learned matched grip. Consequently, I taught myself matched grip outside of classes, because I was passionate about that, but I also took my teacher's passion and learned traditional grip. I found, in the subsequent years, that both had their uses for different styles of music. Now, if I ever get on the kit and play jazz, I always use traditional grip! It is my opinion that the truth lay in between his argument and my perspective and beliefs. But I would never have benefitted from having both techniques if he had not expressed such a strong, complete and passionate argument for traditional. Of course, at the time, I thought he was mental!

So, I urge you to respect your 'opponent's' argument and allow them to express it in full. It also means you will get to lay out your argument fully as well. Additionally, you all need to carry with you the idea that the truth probably lies in between both arguments, although in some more binary decisions it may well be a choice between just one or the other. Do not allow the '3rd way' to pass you by, or get caught in a red mist.

We often take opposing views as personal attacks; because I don't agree with you, it means that I don't really respect you. We need to leave this thinking well behind. Do not shy away from speaking your truth and getting out any points of tension as they appear. If you leave them, or utilise a passive-aggressive approach, then that issue is going to grow. If someone is speaking their mind and has a controversial belief, or maybe is upset with you and is actually telling you to your face, is it possible for you to see this as a compliment? Those who are truthful and tackle the issues head-on are not only stronger as a group, BUT it shows that managing this kind of conflict can also bring you even closer. It is being real with each other. We will not always get on and see things the same, if we did, as the cliché goes, life would indeed be boring!

Let's take two friends – for the sake of the example, we will call them Caz and Emma. Imagine you call Emma up and ask her out to the pub. She says she would love to come but, actually, she is not feeling that great and would rather have a night to chill… Instead, she suggests that you meet on another evening. You then call Caz; she pauses for a bit and then accepts the invitation. When you meet with Caz, she sits there withdrawn and when she does talk, it's about how hard her day was. She is yawning and then starts apologising for her state and eventually you ask if she is tired. Does she want to just go back home? She jumps at the suggestion! She now hates herself for making the decision and for being bad company. How do you think you would feel when you next think of ringing one of these girls again?

When you do next ring Emma, and she says, "Yeh, I am deffo up for a meet up and a drink!" Do you believe her? Yes, of course you do, because when she wasn't up for meeting, she said it outright. Straight down the line! But what of your relationship with Caz? You are now cautious of whether to believe her in many situations, not just in offering to go for a drink with her! **SPEAK YOUR MIND, ALWAYS. Do not try and second-guess what others want to hear. Speak your truth and it will have a profound effect on your life and relationships.**

So, a bit of summary... straight-talking, doing what you say you are going to do and sticking to agreements is the most powerful way of avoiding conflict. Also, if there is a feeling from anyone in the band that they are dissatisfied in some way, then that should be voiced in a straightforward, straight-talking, no skirting round the issue, way.

When we talked about Jim earlier, we suggested that: 'he should call people to the pub and say, with love and compassion, that he has a real issue and wants to sort it. Do not judge that people are acting in a premeditated fashion. It is completely possible and plausible that no one even realises they are acting in such an offensive way.' This is a real rule when you approach your fellow band members, or business people. *Do not make assumptions about others*, we are all full of surprises! Approach these situations from the 'I', not the 'YOU'! You should talk about how 'I feel' and how 'When this happens, I feel/react/act...'. Also, it is very important not to talk about how *'you make me'* – no one *'makes you'* – as a reaction to them; *you make yourself feel!* This refers back to how you can become a victim and once you are in victim mentality, not only is it extremely difficult to move on, but no one, not even you, can help yourself! The issue with victimhood is that you blame someone else for the *way you feel* or what *'happens'* to you, and this means you would need them to help you out of it. You take all power away from yourself to make a change. You see?

The sections on 'looking outside of ourselves' and 'community' is also particularly relevant to conflict resolution and should be revisited with this in mind.

So, here's a list of important markers for conflict resolution:

- **Strong, truthful and respectful communication** – make sure you have had a little breathing/Zone Technique session before approaching these talks. You can use the check-in model from rehearsals and recording.
- **Get rid of the passive-aggressive (but be respectful)!**
- **GIVE to your fellow bandmates – you are one unit, you are family, always look for the greater good NOT personal gain. Look OUTSIDE YOURSELF.**

CHAPTER 13

Setting Up Your Own Staying Sane Local Community Group

Now you have read this book, I strongly advise that you gather together other like-minded musicians and set up a regular support group. It can be monthly, or weekly. Not only can you share and practice the ideas in this book, but you will be supported by your fellow musicians.

Where can you go as a musician where other musicians gather and will listen and understand your struggles exactly?

Here are some guidelines for setting up and running a regular 'Staying Sane' group:

- You will need to encourage people to read this book, of course, so you all have a shared language and understanding of the issues and have begun a practice
- Set up a Facebook group or gather the email addresses of interested members or even a chat group or actually phoning people personally!
- Find a local space that will be private and usable

for 3 hours per week on a weeknight (you may have to ask for very small contributions for the hire space)
- Put chairs in a circle or sit on cushions on the floor
- Light some candles in the middle of the circle and have a sacred speaking object

THE EVENING:

- Open with a short session of 10 minutes of using the Zone Technique just to bring people together into the new space. Someone should call this by ringing a bell or some soft noise to start and stop the session (most phones have this capability!)
- Sharing group – allow anyone to choose to open – invite them to take the speaking object from the centre
- When everyone has shared – break out and have a time where people can go and chat to each other away from the circle
- The second sharing circle will be a discussion on topics that people want to explore – nominate people to bring topics
- Each session someone should be nominated to bring a topic of discussion – present some ideas – this can be discussed in another sharing
- Share ideas in the circle
- Invite speakers on those subjects
- Close the evening with a short use of the Zone Technique for 5 minutes

All free and open discussion should be done on the basis of one person at a time. There should be a chosen 'leader' or two leaders for each week, people who are willing to guide the evening and make sure everyone is being heard and that things run to time.

At the end, you should do a closing circle – everyone gets 1-2 minutes each to feedback about the evening and anything they learned.

By doing this on a regular basis you will become a community. You will share ideas, resources, support each other and become stronger together.

Weekly is best, and of course it doesn't matter if some people can't do it, amongst the group there will always be fluctuation of time patterns, as long as you have even just a group of around 10 people, it will work well.

Pick a night when people are less likely to be gigging and make it a regular weekly meeting on that same day. Be realistic, if it is has to be fortnightly or monthly then so be it. Just try and make it as regular as possible and is realistic.

CONCLUSION
THE FINAL CURTAIN

I mentioned this in Chapter 6; just imagine if you could break every decision you make down into fear or love.

Fear being the place of a weak decision; fear that you are scared, that you are worried, that you are anxious and you are stressed, so you are making a decision from a low place. You are making a decision out of a place of fear. What kind of decision is going to be made from a low place? You are not happy, you may be angry, you feel let down. Are you ever going to be able to make a good decision from this place?

Let's imagine you were on your way to somewhere joyous, like a friend's wedding. Your car breaks down and you are stuck on the side of the motorway waiting for the breakdown service. You are angry, frustrated and upset that you are on the verge of missing your friend's 'once in a lifetime' event. Would you call your friend while you are super upset, given that it's their wedding day, or would you be better off trying to help yourself get into a better mood?

How would you visualise this happening? We all have our own ways of raising our mood. Perhaps you could try and see the humour in the story? Perhaps you could work out how long the breakdown people are going to be, and

> *...Isn't it usual that if you do not overcome the challenges life throws at you, they will come back until you do overcome them?*

whether it is possible that you could make the wedding. Or, that you might miss the ceremony, but you could still get to the party with everyone and be there for your friends to celebrate.

OK, so once you have come to terms with your circumstances, you have dried your tears and you have had some reflection time, you decide that the best thing to do is to send a text to your closest friend at the wedding explaining what has happened, cleverly asking them that if your friend (who is getting married) looks distressed or mentions that you are not there, that this person is designated to explain. Otherwise, you leave it, in the hope that you will get there soon and at least for the party. Can you imagine what would have happened if you had followed a knee-jerk reaction and had decided to call the bride/groom on their wedding day to tell them your shitty story while you were angry, upset and crying?

A place of love is exploration, excitement and GIVING (which is such a big theme), wanting the best for everyone, understanding your true potential, understanding who the others around you are, having your eyes looking outwards not inwards; this is all love.

If you can make every decision from love, you'll be a much better person for it. I hope that you can take all of the ideas in this book and internalise them; this may take quite a few reads! – like you were learning a piece of music – so that you can draw on them any time, and if that means you need to read this book many more times then do it, because it is going to be worth being able to carry these tools with you into your life as a musician. You can also flick back and reread chapters that you need to learn from the most.

To be moving forward with strength, passion, excitement and love in your heart, unlocking your true creative genius, unlocking the words and the creations that you should be saying to the world is your potential.

To be giving to the world wholly and not holding back on your creativity, is your gift.

As I said earlier, it is my belief that you chose the fundamentals of your life.

You chose the circumstances of hardship in your life.

You chose everything you needed to bring the challenges you need to make yourself a better person.

So, believe that the point of life is to overcome the challenges to grow stronger, which then leads to being able to offer our gifts. The more challenges we overcome the better we are at giving unconditionally, because we know ourselves and the nature of life better.

Isn't it usual that if you do not overcome the challenges life throws at you, they will come back until you do overcome them?

So, we chose to come to earth to learn and grow, that earth is the harshest place to learn, there are other planets and environments that we could have gone to, but that earth is the most difficult. We chose to come here, because we felt we would best learn and overcome the challenges we needed to be the most stunning, fantastic souls we can be. In that process, we need to use every gift we have to make this world a better place for all. You are blessed with a skill and joy for music or facilitating those with a talent. So you best use this gift, work with it every day and bring it to us, because here on earth we need you. The universe needs YOU. There is no one else who can be the exact you with all your perfect imperfections.

YES!

The struggle is the challenge and the challenge is a gift for us to grow.

To find out more, book Brett for speaking engagements or workshops please email - **info@stayingsane.org**

For more info
www.stayingsane.org

Thank you to Sound Disposition - Roland Heap and Tom Beale for amazing work on the audio book.

Thanks to Dave Mitchell for Being my partner in the band 'Samba Tigers' and for the use of small excerpts in the audio book version!

Thanks to David Stillitz for Additional Materials.

Thanks to James and all the team at SpiffingCovers.

Diplomats of Sound Artist Development Agency

In my day job I run Diplomats of Sound CIC, a not-for-profit artist development agency, with Si Chai (founder of Chai Wallahs and Diplomats of Sound Booking Agency). Our development agency sits in between Chai Wallahs Festival Venue and the Diplomats of Sound Booking Agency. Our aim is to help artists to develop in both profile and strategy.

Through our experience and knowledge of the marketplace in the digital age, we have precisely isolated the areas that artists need to have perfected in order to break into the market and become professional. In today's world the two key elements required are the constant implementation of a social media strategy, along with a solid management strategy, timeline and a clear set of goals for releases, touring, recording, logistics, image, design and band dynamics.

On-Demand Management:

Do you often find yourselves saying "we need a manager" There is an extreme shortage of music managers with experience, integrity and honesty. What's more, the cost to develop a band and launch them into the marketplace is high and is usually a high-risk, competitive and costly process.In general, many creatively minded people lack the necessary organisational skills and music business/industry knowledge. Unfortunately, the type of people that possess those skills can be extremely money motivated.

The advantage for the artist in today's digital age is that

there are now multiple ways in which you can manage yourselves. There is no longer a dependence on a manager to unlock doors in getting a label, distribution or publishing deal or, more importantly, actually getting your songs heard by the public, being able to create a buzz and growing an audience. This can all be done by YOU and bands left, right and centre are doing exactly that THEMSELVES.

However, what you do need is sound advice, including a clear management strategy, a clear set of achievable/realistic goals, solid structure, legal advice, and access to a wealth of knowledge and experience in the minefield that is the music industry.

Our coaching will help you navigate the choppy waters of the music industry and music marketplace, protecting your creative rights, helping increase your profile and income, avoiding the pitfalls, whilst increasing your awareness and knowledge of the options and choices you can make to achieve your goals/aims.

All the while, every step you take with us, we will be educating you on the music business. So you will become capable of steering your ship and you will gain experience in job roles and expectations. This means, as your business grows and business personnel join, you are able to make sound decisions and look out for the interests of you, your band and other colleagues, without getting ripped off!

Between our directors we have 50+ years of experience in all aspects of the music industry. We have all chosen to spend our time nurturing fresh talent because that is our passion. We have our eye keenly focused on the musician's perspective, whilst having a huge network of industry pros, and have worked with a host of bands that have gone on to achieve their goals.

This is cheaper than traditional management, as you only pay for what you use rather than having a manager fobbing you off on a retainer (20% of all your gig money and other income) and not pulling their weight. This is a transparent service and we pride ourselves on only happy customers/ musicians.

Our Services Include (but are not limited to):

Development of Strategy
Coaching, Strategy, Organisation into manageable steps:
Two-hour coaching, consultancy, strategy and organisation service – You have the opportunity of working with a professional who can guide you with this bespoke service. You will walk away with a clear plan for the next 6 months - 1 year of work (depending on your level).

Live Performance and Stage Presentation Workshop:
Four-hour rehearsal critique – We come to your rehearsal where you perform as if you were playing a live show. We then break down your set and critique the presentation and performance including, but not limited to, the composition, set order, and parts that are being played by each member of the band. We then make suggestions on every aspect of the performance that needs improvement so that you come across as a confident, professional and experienced live act. We can literally shave years off of your development process in one session!

Three in-depth workshop sessions – In this 3-workshop period, we break your band down to the bare bones and help you to build it back up… analysing and tweaking every aspect/section, track and instrument in order to help each individual express their full potential. This will include technical advice, all the aspects mentioned above in the 4-hour critique, but this is a much more detailed process. We will leave you sounding pro; this is a fast-track system to blow your audience away at every live show and transform your level.

We have witnessed over 3,500 performances, in a wide variety of genres, in front of a multitude of audiences. We have seen what works, what doesn't, and what makes some artists stand out from the rest/shine. We understand audiences, the industry and your marketplace. We give you the pro angle, which only stage experience can normally teach you. But, we will help hone your presentation and give you the awareness and guidance that will fast-track you and make you appear that you have been playing stages for many more years than you have!

Legal Services

We can provide legal advice and documents for band agreements, record and publishing deals, sponsorship opportunities, distribution, media, copyright, IP, and song splits with producers and writers.

We can also review and negotiate, or even renegotiate existing contracts.

Conflict Resolution

We act as mediators, we can help resolve disagreements with music businesses, band members, management or any other contractual issues you might have.

Professional Representation

To instil confidence and to prevent you from getting 'your pants pulled down!' you can call upon us to represent you in industry meetings.

We will meet with you in advance to discuss aims, objectives and potential strategies before creating a deal outline that defines the boundaries of an acceptable agreement with a third party company.

(Fee to be worked on the specific scenario.)

We are essentially an 'on-demand' management service and a 'Citizens' Advice Bureau' for musicians.

If you are interested in any of these services or want to book Brett for speaking engagements/media/press you can contact me here:

brett@diplomatsofsound.org

Thanks

I am dedicating this book to all the amazing people in my life that have helped shape me as a human, called me out on my bullshit, forgave me for my mistakes and acted as a mirror for me to see and help me to understand my shadow.

Love and support to my beautiful partner, Emma (Dr Pixie WonderWoman). Our love is new, but your support and loyalty is strong and you are an exceptional being of light and giving, and I look forward to our future together.

Many parts of this book were written with the help of the album Carboot Soul by Nightmares on Wax – Thanks to George Evelyn for creating such an amazing album! Bruce Wood for introducing me to the album, particular solace in 'Morse', coffee and a morning, peaceful drum set ups at the amazing and zen Touchwood Audio Production Studios, Hyde Park, Leeds.

Special thanks to all the thought leaders who have influenced my life and beliefs: David Deida, Alex Vartman, Diesel, Paris and all the TNT teachers and TNT friends. To my ManKind Warrior Brothers and most recently Rod Boothroyd for love, support and amazing teachings through difficult times. And… for life wisdoms – Grant Leboff, Rabbi Lord Jonathan Sacks, Aryeh Kaplan, Rabbi Baruch and Kezi Levin, Yosef Solomon, Jordan Peterson, Joe Rogan, Alan Watts, Ken Wilber, Louis CK, Bill Bailey, Rowan Atkinson, Prince, Michael Jackson and many more which would take an entire page to thank!

Very special, unbelievable thanks to, my parents, Penny for overcoming incredible adversity so many times and

Dad, Ashley Leboff, who took on the unbelievable task of helping raise me from being an out of control kid and has been a light and a blessing, and for both of your love, support and belief. For proof reading and ideas. My brothers, their wives and children, Grant for your exceptional marketing, business advice, ideas on life and work opportunities, and Julie, Dena, Dylan, Ethan, and Ari, love you all so much, Amanda and Jeremy, for your unwavering support, love and encouragement, Barney and Alfie you all Rock! and, of course, David Stillitz brother from another mother, for your love and support, through thick and thin.

Jonathan Silverman, for patience and teaching, I learned a lot that year and was also beginning a journey of, arguably, the most challenging 5 years of my life!

Len Bendel, my lawyer, business partner for some time, generosity of time, voice of reason, Zen teacher and one who I could not be where I am today without.

My ex-wife, Anick Landau, who helped me on a long, dark and much-needed personal development path, with patience, love and respect.

Si Chai – for incredible mentoring, belief and trust in me, and giving me the opportunities I need to grow as a person and professionally.

Tom Toast – for believing in me and inviting/welcoming me into the community.

Charles Kennedy – for constant support in my career, some of the funniest times I have had in my career, love, support, 'pants-off Fridays', incredible optimism and belief in this book.

Geezer Danny O'Neil – daily office banter, amazing times over a period of years, fun chats, red wine and jazz funk!

Chris Hampshire (Massive Massive Massive) – Amazing support, hours of phone conversations, the gift of DJ Avis Van Rental that kept me sane in difficult times. Some of the best times I have had in my music career and the best stories are down to you my friend!

Jennie and Jonathan Wallace – Jen, you have been a rock all the way through my career. An amazing support, huge encouragement, massive help with branding, websites and helping me deal with the pitfalls of self-promotion. Without you, I would struggle! Thanks sooo much for everything! You are an angel.

All the Diplomats' Agents Crew and Chai Wallahs Crew you are all totally awesome, I joined you in a delicate and fragile state and you made me feel part of the family. So, big ups!

Chay Honey – for welcoming me and letting me be your bitch!

Dean James Barratt – for bringing me the opportunity to take on the big boys! Believing, loyalty, helping my development, being an absolute legend and for an incredible amount of laughs.

Trenton Birch – for being an inspiration and helping inspire and shape me at the beginning of my management career.

Oded Kafri – for journeying with me through the biggest years of transformation in my life, teaching me, being a case study!

Dan Shinder – for being a legend, a teacher and managing to sustain smile and laughter more than most I know.

Hendicott! – for encouragement, love and spiritual know-how.

Jop/Joshi, whatever your name is! – For an exceptional enthusiasm, love and unwavering belief in me.

Tucker – for being a legend, and all the years of amazing

work and goodness.

Holly Holden Y Su Banda! Super group of people and a pleasure to work with, I believe in you.

Dan Raff – for booking my bands way back, welcoming me into your world, support in this project and for your programming – Shambala Festival positively changed the course of my life!

Old UKTI crew, AIM, MMF and BPI people Brian Message, Phil Patteson, Pippa McEvoy & Sybil Bell, Becky Ayres, for guidance and support and all those that I met at the beginning of my career, when I was juvenile, young, green and a wally! All the people I was on trade missions with, was an idiot around, thanks and sorry if I was way too much, fickle and an idiot.

Tom Hawkins and Nick Barbian, thanks for working with me in Monumental Management, the time and dedication you showed was incredible and you were both outstanding team players. Thanks also for putting up with a rookie boss!

Rudey and Q for being great team members and dealing with my bad humour and mistakes.

Cleeve and Jess, Tali and Dan, Bronya and Chris, Rachel Rose Reid and you and Joel Stanley welcoming me into one of the best communities ever!, Nicole S, Nikki Nikster Sparkle Queen, Incredible support, loyalty and coaching through hard times.

All you lot who have helped me to become the person I am, encouraged silliness and focus…Amazing Vessels crew and amazing, actual WAGs – Pete and J, Lee and Anna, Martin and Orsi Tom & Trina, Tim and Elise, Oli and Nadine, Murg and Eve, Helen, Matt and Rach, Ben, Rach, and my godson, Bruce, Simon and Kathryn, Austin for giving and keeping us safe! Dave Smith for providing a community environment of learning and development, great food and a nurturing attitude and those infamous long days of Risk! Paddy and Margeax. Billy Laurance, for being a Zen legend, all the old Thelonious crew, all the old Doctor Octopus crew, including groupies ;) Trumpet 'Easy' Dave you were there for all of it! The Neil Innes! Harry Marin, Jon and Weenie, Georgie and Dan, Sally, Marsha and Stuart, Jez and Romy, Nikster and Daz, Stephen Hopper, Bill Wadhams, Rochelle Levy, new no.59 crew George, Jonny and Adam, Rails and Tilly, Jimbo and Claire, Sal, Lyndsay, Christo and Benny, you all rock. Jo Jo Cohen, Yosef Solomon and family for love, light and wisdom, Japanese crew Yuki, Miki and all you beautiful souls that held me when I was seeing you regularly in your wonderful land! The Middle-earth connections – Professor Aviad Hadar, the Right Reverend David Rachmani, the retired commando Shaul 'Zamshid' Shwimmer and Karin Keren, Julia Levy, the spiritual warrior Jamie Gordon. Lou Lou for friendship, love and support in uni days, Lana and Shai, Rochelle and Dan, Laura Moss for connection and our shared love of Prince! All original Leeds crew from 221 Hyde Park Road and 245 Hyde Park Road, you were all exceptionally patient with me and showed a lot of love. FILTHY kicks Crew being able to play in the band while managing was so much fun, you guys all rock, you brought much joy during a much needed time of my stressful music management job! Russell and Jamie Warren, Ray and Ruth Upwood, Watford FC !!!

All my TNT friends Dom or Hangover or whatever your name is, thanks for inspiration for some of this. Waaaaay too many other friends, who are my family and have been for the last 20 years, all the Leeds crew, London 'back in the day' crew, Moish crew, you all know exactly who you are, I love you all dearly, you have always offered me support, encouragement, allowed me to be completely mental, talk my mind, talk way too much, dealt with me being a complete idiot and not holding grudges. Without ALL of my friends and the people above, there is no way, I would have the belief and motivation to write these words.

Lastly, all the artists in bands and in management that I have worked with, you have all helped shape me as a human and taught me so much about the struggles and glory of a professional musician's existence. Including Animotion, Arrival Soundsystem, ATA Records, Big Strides Blatantly Blunt, Broken Brass Ensemble, Brotherly, Cable Street Collective, Claire Northey, Dean James Barrett, Dojo, Faeland, Feelgood Experiment, Foodoo, FABRIK, Gabby Young, Gypsy Hill, Holly Holden (Y Su Banda), IAMU, Ian Britt, Jess McAllister, JD73, The Jazz Defenders, KAFRi & Drum The World, KOKOROKO, Lana, Pat Dam Smith, Rusangano Family, Simon McCorry, Smash Hifi, Solana, Solomon O.B & The Sankofa 3, Time for T, Trenton & Free Radical, The Baghdaddies Urband Soul, Vessels, Yael Deckelbaum, Yumi & The Weather.

Thank you also to Grandmas and Grandpas and Aunts and Uncles.

Additional Thank Yous: Clive Selwyn, Oriel Poole, Melissa Abercassis, Mark & Bella Partridge, Rich, Amy, Karig & Maeve Ely, Deborah Curtis, Ian Britt